CURIOUS ALIGNMENTS:
THE GLOBAL ECONOMY
SINCE 2500 BCE

By Dr. John Sase, Ph.D.

Edited by Gerard J. Senick

Curious Alignments:
The Global Economy since 2500 BCE,
An Exploration into the Pre-History of Urban Areas, Land Use, and Geodesy
from the Bronze Age through the Age of Exploration
ISBN: 1449567738
EAN-13: 9781449567736

A Project of Kavish Media Group Economic Series
SASE Associates
by
John F. Sase, Ph.D.

Address inquiries to
drjohn@saseassociates.com
SASE Associates
27350 Southfield Rd. PMB 170
Lathrup Village, MI 48076

TABLE OF CONTENTS

PREFACE FOR JOHN'S BOOK BY BOB FRITCHIE

The locations of many sacred sites have been known for centuries. Each site has played a major role in the development of the people who live in the local region near where the site was constructed. What is apparent from this book is that all of these sites were interconnected. As Dr. Sase carries us through the development of the geometry used to align these sites, the reader is struck by several incontrovertible truths:

- Ancient civilizations must have possessed advanced navigational capabilities to align all of these sites precisely into a worldwide grid.

- The placement of sacred sites must have been coordinated.

- The resulting grid cannot be mere coincidence.

As we move towards a better understanding of the present and the past, humankind has a renewed opportunity to decode the messages associated with these sacred sites. I recall a lecture in 1980 by the eminent scientist Dr. Marcel Vogel, a researcher at IBM, who said, "Records are written in stone." He was referring to energetic messages. Vogel had decoded an ancient civilization from a rock that he had been given. Research by several major companies has validated Vogel's earlier revelation: thoughts or electronic records can be transferred energetically into various materials.

Hence we are left to ponder even more intriguing possibilities:

- Did the ancient civilizations communicate with each other around the world? Did they share information? If so, how was that done?

- Did these civilizations record their evolving history in stone artifacts at sacred sites?

- Perhaps the information developed at each sacred site was given from advanced civilizations on other planetary systems. If this is the case, then we all may be awakening to greater truths.

- What will be the benefit to humankind in rediscovering and applying these ancient spiritual and physical truths?

Curious Alignments is a major work that deserves close study by the public and academicians everywhere.

Robert G. Fritchie
Director
World Service Institute
P.O. Box 32801
Knoxville, TN 37930
www.worldserviceinstitute.org

INTRODUCTION:

As I look out my kitchen window, I see two trees that have lived in my backyard for many years and a cement pedestal bird bath that I placed in the yard a number of years ago. In deciding where to put this bird bath, I measured the distance between the two trees and used that length to form an equilateral triangle. The trees secured two of the corners and the bird bath marked the third point. In effect, I took a phenomenon of nature (or at least the effort of a previous property owner) and combined it with my own location preference, using a basic element of ancient geometry to complete a simple relationship between human thought and divine nature.

In the modern world, urban and regional site selection, planning, design, and construction of edifices may not appear to reflect a divine process. However, in the ancient and medieval worlds, the Divine often inspired these practical plans and actions in a way conjoined with the mystical aspects of religion. The layout of a particular camp, village, or city, the direction in which an edifice faced, the time and place that the sun shined through a main entranceway or window, and the placement of ceremonial altars and fountains held great significance for the humans involved in the process. The Sacred Geometry that produced pleasing aesthetics for the eye also produced perfect acoustics for the ear. These qualities inspire awe. In addition, ritual chanting continues to move site visitors deeply to the present day.

Divine design was not only reflected in the construction of these holy places. The site selections of these places in relationship to one another often mirrored the alignment of planets and stars in the heavens—as above, so below. The human desire to understand the cosmos extends back to ages for which we possess no records except the ceremonial sites themselves and the Sacred Geometry reflected within and among them. Considering the known or estimated dates at which many sacred sites were constructed, it appears that the use of Sacred Geometry--the geometry used to design sacred art and architecture that comes from the metaphysical study of the nature of the universe--has waxed and waned multiple times over successive millennia of our epoch. In various parts of the world, the construction of pyramids, stone circles, mounds, and temples sometimes transpired concurrently. Sometimes it did not.

Furthermore, the use of Sacred Geometry has focused on the movements of the sun, moon, stars and planets for reasons extending from the purely pragmatic to the completely spiritual. This is true for the most primitive and pagan of cultures to the most advanced and traditional of societies. In respect to the latter, let us consider this first example.

Many moviegoers who have watched the 1972 Franco Zeffirelli film *Brother Sun, Sister Moon* (1972) identify the title with Saint Francis and Saint Clare of Assisi, Italy. However, during the revival of the science and art of Sacred Geometry in architecture in the thirteenth and fourteenth centuries, medieval Christians thought that Saint John the Baptist and Mary Magdalene more often personified the sun and the moon. As a result, many holy sites of the time were dedicated to Saint John and the Magdalene. Cathedrals and churches incorporated Sacred Geometry to announce the most relevant days of solar and lunar activity. The structures have stood not only as places to conduct ceremonies, but as places to preserve ancient science and mathematics in the architecture. For example, during the centuries before an abundance of mechanical clocks, the brass strip known as the Roseline embedded in the floor of the Church of Saint-Sulpice in Paris was used to reflect sunlight as a call to noon service.

THE ROSELINE AT SAINT SULPICE

Over the past two centuries, those of us on the American continents have discovered numerous sites and structures that embody the same Sacred Geometry. Some of these sacred sites stand as stone pyramids that reflect the geometry found in the structure of pyramids in Egypt, Mesopotamia, and elsewhere. Meanwhile, other sites survive as packed-earth or clay-brick mounds. While some of these structures embody the shape and dimensions of the stone pyramids, others do not. Secondly, a multitude of stone circles exist throughout the world. Of those studied, a large number appear to possess placement, spacing, and alignments similar to the best-known ancient stone circles in the British Isles. Finally, investigators have noticed connections among the multiple placements of many structures that follow the principles of Sacred Geometry.

In my own investigation of these curiosities, I began my journey toward enlightenment by studying ancient American sites in the Midwestern states of Michigan and Ohio. From my home base in Michigan, I searched far and wide to locate sites and discover alignments along with other pertinent features. The further I delved, the more mysterious that I found these curiosities. Consequently, I have located, marked, and mapped the curiosities that I found. I invite you to journey with me and explore the mysteries that loom beneath these curious alignments. Within these mysteries, we will find that applied Sacred Geometry exists as a highly conscious melding of science, art, and magic. In other words, this application was no mere leisure activity for our early ancestors. It appears that they used Sacred Geometry to help them to survive daily life.

Chapter 1
THE OLD COPPER CULTURE

Named by archeologists as the "Old Copper Culture," the first indigenous peoples who mined and utilized copper flourished in upper Michigan from 5000 BCE to 700 CE. These miners left few burial grounds, dwellings, pottery, clay tablets, or cave drawings. However, they did leave behind thousands of copper-producing pits and the crude hammering stones with which they worked. Apparently, these ancient miners worked the copper-bearing rock by alternately applying fire and cold water by using stone hatchets or hand-held hammering stones. This technique allowed them to break the ore into smaller pieces from which they could extract the metal. From this copper, they formed additional tools.

We continue to know very little about the proliferation of Neolithic copper mines that rim the western part of Lake Superior. Our first verification that these copper mines stemmed from the aforementioned ancient dates came from scientific proof in 1954. Dr. Roy W. Drier, a metallurgical engineer on the faculty of what is now known as Michigan Technical University in Houghton, received a grant from the Wenner-Gren Foundation that allowed him to lead an expedition to Isle Royale for the purpose of obtaining and studying specimens of organic matter taken from abandoned mine pits. Employing the then-new Carbon 14 dating process, two measurements resulted that dated these pits to between 1800 and 1000 BCE. From this expedition, Drier reported the existence of more than 2,000 pits in the area along the Minong belt around the lakeshore and on scattered islands of Lake Superior.

At this point, we should note that the date of 1800 BC falls within the Twelfth Dynasty of Egypt, the apex, and the most stable period of, the Middle Kingdom. The dynasty originally centered in the city of Thebes, which stands on the Nile approximately halfway between the Pyramids of Giza and the Abu Simbel Temple further upriver. In building the pyramids at Giza and the temples and palaces at Abu Simbel, Karnak, and elsewhere, master builders needed an endless supply of copper saws, chisels, and hammers in the limestone quarries at the construction sites. Why is this important? These coincidences may prove to be a key element to solving this mystery. However, let us not jump to conclusions. Rather, let us store this thought in the back of our minds as we progress.

The earliest known modern writings concerning the copper region of Michigan came in 1665 when Jesuit missionaries Jean LeSeur and Claude Dablon reported that copper existed in vast quantities along the shore of Lake Superior. These mineral finds drew the governments of France, England, and other European countries to explore and lay claim to this territory. Finally, the Chippewa Tribe ceded all claims to 30,000 square miles of the Upper Peninsula to the United States Government in 1842. As a result, the Copper Rush of 1843 commenced, as thousands of would-be miners came to the Copper Country to try their luck.

Throughout the latter half of the nineteenth century, commercial extraction of copper burgeoned in the area. These mines helped to build the prosperity of the city of Duluth, Minnesota, and towns eastward along the south shore of Lake Superior in Michigan. John Jacob Houghton, one of the early leading figures in the Copper Country, produced his piece *The Ancient Copper Mines of Lake Superior* (1879). He wrote, "On the south shore of Lake Superior, the works of the ancient miners extend over a district… comprising… a length of one hundred and fifty miles through Keenenaw, Houghton and Octonagon Counties, Michigan, with a varying width of from four to seven miles." By the end of the nineteenth century, the shafts of

Keweenaw were the deepest in the world. However, when the mines no longer proved profitable, the companies and employees left. Today, the ruins of mines and ghost towns are what you see. However, there still remains an abundance of copper.

Copper deposits appear on every continent of the world in greater or lesser amounts,. In ancient times, the mining of copper took place on the Sinai Peninsula; on the island of Cyprus; in the countries of Spain, China, Mexico, and Peru; and in the region surrounding Lake Superior. Of the more extensive copper ore deposits in the world, four major sites exist in the Rocky Mountains and great basin in the western United States, the length of the Andean chain in Peru, in Northern Rhodesia and on the central plateau in Africa, and in central Canada extending south into the Upper Peninsula of Michigan.

Where did the extracted copper go? Some scholars believe that Phoenician explorers, Berbers, Bronze Age Europeans, and/or Norsemen may have mined the majority of it within a huge international trading center on the shores of Lake Superior. During the Bronze Age, the demand for copper throughout the ancient world hit a peak.

Through built much later than the Egyptian structures, the walls of Sacsayhuaman and the Palace of Manco Capac at Cuzco, Peru (400 through 1200 CE) resemble those in Giza. For example, polished copper plate entirely covered the interior of Coricancha. Apart from minor differences, artisans decorated the Temple of the Sun at Cuzco in the same manner as the interior of the Treasury of Atreus in Mycenae, Greece (1250 BCE). Contemporaneous with the Mycenae, the Chavin culture in Peru flourished from 1200 BC to 200 BC. Furthermore, archeologists digging in Peru have unearthed bronze figures, dating from 1523 to 1027 BCE, that resemble ones associated with the Shang dynasty in China. Near the city of Xi'an, approximately 100 mound pyramids remain standing, having been built between 2000 and 21 BCE. These Chinese pyramids resemble the many mound pyramids discovered throughout the Americas and other parts of the world.

REMAINS OF THE TEMPLE OF THE SUN AT CUZCO

In North and Central America, various mounds and pyramids made of earth, clay brick, and stone remain throughout the continent. The most abundant concentrations of these structures survive in southern Michigan and southern Ohio. In fact, thirty thousand mounds lay scattered throughout a restricted area of Ohio. Analysis of the large Seip mound,[1] which stands 240 feet long, 130 feet wide, and thirty feet high in Ross County, renders a Carbon 14 reading of 300 BCE.

---

[1] (39° 14' 16" N at 83° 13' 13" W)

Near Peterborough, Ontario, Canada,[2] one can find several hundred petroglyphs that date from 1500 BCE. The late Dr. H. B. "Barry" Fell, professor emeritus of Harvard, recognized that that both the script and picture carvings on the glyphs resembled an ancient Germanic language used by the Scandinavians during the Bronze Age around 2500 BCE. Fells noted that petroglyphs similar to the ones in Ontario also have been found in Norway and Sweden. Seemingly related to these petroglyphs, inscriptions on a forty-by-seventy foot white limestone rock located northeast of Toronto tell of a Norseman king named Woden-lithi who sailed on a trading mission to America around 1500 BCE for ingot copper of excellent quality.

Concurrently, ancient civilizations flourished in the valley of the Indus River system in the region now known as Pakistan. Thirty sites containing lost cities and villages, such as the city of Mohenjo Daro[3] that was discovered 300 miles north of Karachi, date from 5000 to 1500 BCE. Another site at Harrapa, near the Ravi River, flourished from 2700 BC to 2300 BCE.

In Europe, north of Scotland across the Pentland Firth, a Bronze Age culture inhabited the Orkney Islands around 4000 BCE. These prehistoric people built stone houses along with solar-, and lunar-oriented megalithic monuments well before the first Egyptian dynasty. The Neolithic (early Bronze Age) civilization of the Orkneys grew, expanded, and faded out over the course of thousands of years. Near Skae Brae, visitors still find the Standing Stones of Stenness and the Ring of Brodgar—thirty-six stones standing up to fifteen feet high. Nearby, one finds the ring temple of Maes Howe. This temple was built from massive stone slabs, each weighing as much as thirty tons. On the day of Winter Solstice, the sunlight enters between the stones and

---

[2] (44° 18′ N at 78° 19′ W)

[3] (27° 19′ N at 68° 8′ E)

passes through a doorway of the temple. Contemporaneous with these sites, a nearby culture in New Grange ("new sun"), Ireland, built a highly accurate solar calculator around 3000 BCE.

STANDING STONES OF STENNESS

The mound-building period began after 3500 BCE. The first Egyptian dynasties built pyramids by using sun-dried mud brick around 3100 BCE. Within 600 years, builders used the same type of brick in the first South American pyramid complexes in Caral and Tucume, Peru, in approximately 2500 BCE. Dr. Ruth Shady Solis, a Peruvian archeologist and lead investigator of Caral, has worked on this project for many years.

Carbon 14 tests of the remains of woven reed bags, possibly used to carry stones, provide a date estimate of 3600 BCE for these pyramids. This legacy continued in the Americas. From year 0 to 700 CE, the Moche culture of Peru built mud-brick adobe pyramids. The Mayans built pyramids at Comalcalco made of clay mixed with sand and dried oyster shells about 600 to 900 CE. In further reference to Egyptian structures, the Pyramid of the Sun at Teotihuacan, Mexico (100 CE), has a base of 44,000 square meters, one that sets nearly identical to that of the Cheops (Khufu) pyramid at Giza.

In regions now that are part of the United States, ancient inhabitants constructed a vast number of stone circles and mounds. In addition, these Bronze Age cultures built mounds and pyramids. However, the local lack of stone often dictated the use of clay or soil in the construction. As the Egyptians built their first step pyramids around 3000 BCE, Native Americans in the lower Mississippi Valley built their community surrounded by earthen mound pyramids. Similarly, a later culture that flourished from 1500 to 600 BCE in Poverty Point, Louisiana,[4] built a large number of concentric, semi-circular mounds bordered by large conical mounds. Their great bird-shaped mound stands at the center of this complex.

MISSISSIPPI MOUNDS

Bronze Age cultures constructed earthen mounds, clay and stone pyramids, and stone circles in all sizes and shapes throughout the world. Sites include India, New Guinea, Germany, Russia, Poland, France, England, and elsewhere. Furthermore, evidence that large mounds and pyramids

---

[4] (32°38′ N at 91°24′ W)

possessing similar alignments to one another suggests that they had an astronomical use. Many of the structures orientate toward the Solstice points along the horizon (points of sunrise and sunset at Summer and Winter Solstice) and the points of the rising and setting moon at the furthest distance of the moon from the ecliptic (the major and minor moon rises and settings).

Also, many of these structures have point toward certain fixed stars. At the Mayan site at Uaxactum, Guatemala, three temples, along with two steles (upright stones or slabs with inscribed or sculptured surfaces), provide the exact orientations of the sun's position during solstices and equinoxes. At Teotihuacan near Mexico City,[5] a series of stone markers line up with the Pyramid of the Sun to indicate the rising and setting sun at solstices and equinoxes. The great pyramid of Xochicalc[6] casts a precise, round shadow twice each year when shining down a vertical shaft with the sun at its peak. In Hovenweep Castle, an ancient Anasazi ruin near the Colorado-Utah border that was built between 1150 and 1200 CE, a chosen room served as a solar observatory. Several holes cut into the walls align with the rays of the sun at particular times of the year, specifically the Summer and Winter Solstices and spring and fall equinoxes.

---

[5] (19°41'39.31"N at 98°52'9.70"W)
[6] (18° 48' 14" N at 99° 17' 47" W)

Chapter 2
BRONZE AGE MEASUREMENT

"They discuss and teach youths about the heavenly bodies and their motions, the dimensions of the world and of countries, natural science and the powers of the immortal gods."
                    --Julius Caesar, commenting on the British Druids

During the Bronze Age, the conception and construction of pyramids and related structures required a working knowledge and the use of the square, triangle, circle, and five-sided pentangle. As a result, a number of questions arise.

In their book *The Lost Science of Measuring the Earth: Discovering the Sacred Geometry of the Ancients* (Adventures Unlimited Press, 2006), Robin Heath and John Michell ask the following series of questions:

- Did prehistoric people measure length and distances accurately? If they did, how did they do so?
- Where are their rods or ropes? How did they maintain a standard of length?
- How could an agrarian tribal society that ate from crude pots become so motivated as to accurately measure angles or long lengths over terrain that was often rugged?
- How was it possible to determine the size of the earth? Could prehistoric surveyors have measured latitude and longitude?

These queries constitute important and relevant questions as we proceed in our quest of curious alignments and the mysteries that lie beneath them. The epoch for discovering and unraveling the science of surveying and geodetics extends over the past four or five thousand years. In terms of geography, we can look to the age of ancient Greece during the sixth century BCE. In respect to that age, orthodox historical records credit Anaximander with the distinction of inventing maps. Within a century of that invention, Thales of Miletus announced that the earth was spherical.

However, modern thought often argues that the ideas of the ancient Greeks were based upon philosophy rather than on facts gained from observation or experimentation. If this is so, then Robin Heath and John Michell wonder consequently why the ancient figures for the size of the Earth prove so astonishingly accurate. In their book, the authors suggest that the Greeks derived their source from precision measurements.

Neal and Michell state two basic axioms for understanding ancient measurement systems: Ancient units of length are grouped into "families" connected to one another via whole number ratios and based on a root measure whose length is always related to the measure of a foot, and these "families" of units form exact fractions of one of the three principal dimensions of the Earth—the polar radius, the meridian circumference (the circle passing through the north and south poles), and the equatorial circumference of the Earth.

In respect to these axioms, let us consider the work of Claudius Ptolemy, the Greco-Roman geographer who lived in the second century CE. Ptolemy calculated a one-degree arc of the Earth in a measure that converts to 69.12 English furlong miles. His measurement remains the current value for one degree at the meridian circumference, the one from which our nautical mile is derived. Furthermore, the first-century Roman philosopher and geographer Pliny the Elder calculated the polar radius (center of the Earth to the pole) as being a measure that converts exactly to 3,949.71 miles--a figure almost identical to our modern estimate.

As all of us learned (and many of us forgot) in elementary school, the earth is not a true sphere. Rather, it is an ellipsoid, bulging at the equator. Subsequently, in his book *Ancient Metrology* (Pentacle Books, 1981), John Michell identified the ancient measure of the meridian circumference as being equal to our present-day number of 24,883.2 miles. This suggests that the ancients possessed the knowledge of this peculiarity. In addition, Heath and Michell proceed to demonstrate in *The Lost Science of Measuring the Earth* that ancient Egyptian, Greek, and Roman measurements all produce very precise determinations of this same circumference. Bottom line? The great minds of 2,000 years ago not only understood that the Earth is round, but they were able to measure its size accurately. In fact, Sir Isaac Newton employed the Egyptian Sacred Cubit (about 2.07 English feet) to obtain his own figure for the size of the Earth in the seventeenth century.

To measure the latitude of the Earth, first we must accept that the Earth is spherical. Based on this premise, our task remains to measure the Culmination Angles of the stars (these being the highest points observed as we look due south) accurately. Though currently we do not know what methods or instruments were used by ancient cultures, the locations of many sacred sites around the world suggest that the placement of these sites was more than accidental. In support of this hypothesis, the Scottish engineer Dr. Alexander Thom demonstrated that those who built Stonehenge could split a "minute of arc" (as in degree, minutes, and seconds). He stated in a BBC television interview in 1970, "That's better than what can be done in modern surveying."

To measure the difference in north-south longitude between any two points on the Earth requires two conditions: Both observers must establish the same moment in time — synchronicity--and they must make their observations of the sky at two different locations, simultaneously. One simple technique that that Bronze Age humans could have discovered and used relies upon the observation of the first moment of the earth's shadow across a full moon during a lunar eclipse. This moment varies by position of longitude in a way that is measurable by the naked human eye. As with latitude, the accurate measurement of angles is necessary for calculating the difference between longitudes.

In our modern age, we know that the most accurate measurement of angles comes from the development of trigonometry. Heath and Michell point out that "some of the earliest cuneiform tablets from Babylonia demonstrate that the required trigonometry was established prior to 2000 BC[E]…. The ancients were well nigh obsessed with the measurement of angles and research into geometry—a word which today is often taken to mean the creation and analysis of shapes, yet actually means 'measuring the world'; Geo-metry."

Therefore, given the root measure (such as a foot or cubit) of any of the number of ancient linear measurement systems, and given the principal dimensions of the Earth, the resulting measures and dimensions would serve to establish the relationship between any set of temples, pyramids, or mounds. Furthermore, these measures and dimensions would serve to establish the distances between these structures and the location on the planet at which they have been placed—a relatively heavy thought. Heath and Michell describe the use of these measures and dimensions as "applied Sacred Geometry, a high consciousness meld of science, art, and magic." In other words, this is not a mere leisure activity. It appears that ancient cultures used some form of Sacred Geometry to help them to survive everyday life. Their basic geometry allowed them to track the movement of the sun, the moon, and the five visible planets against the night sky with accuracy. In turn, they used their observations to calculate the time to plant, gather, hunt, and fish. Furthermore, such knowledge of time, place, and changes allowed them to monitor and predict major changes in climate that would force them to migrate closer to the equator. Finally, their command of Sacred Geometry provided them with the means to communicate with their deities. As a result, applied Sacred Geometry constitutes the tool that we will use to explore the curious alignments of the Earth and the mysteries that lie beyond them.

From our study of ancient surveying and geodetics, we arrive at an understanding of the placement of various ancient temples, pyramids, and mounds around the world. For example, the Egyptians built the Pyramids of Giza at the latitude of thirty degrees, north.[7] This location marks a point that sits at one-third of the distance from the equator to the North Pole and marks the midpoint of the land masses of the planet. In addition, Thebes,[8] the capital city of the Old Kingdom of Egypt, and Avebury Henge in England[9] are situated precisely at points that measure two-sevenths and four-sevenths of the distance from equator to pole, respectively. In Thebes, Egypt, the Temple of Amun constituted the geodetic center from which all distances in the kingdom were measured. In Avebury, England, the latitude band calculated as 360/7 passes through the middle of the henge and its ruined stone circle—known as the largest in the world.

---

[7] (Cheops, the largest, sits at 29° 58′ 45″ N, less than a mile-and-a-half south of 30 degrees latitude)
[8] (25° 41′ 60″ N at 32° 34′ 60″ E)
[9] (51° 25′ 43″ N at 1° 51′ 14″ W)

AVEBURY HENGE

Chapter 3
THE OLD HOW-TO

"How could it be possible for a Neolithic Society to have engineered the monuments we find today?"
--T. B. Pawlicki, "Megalithic Engineering: How to Build Stonehenge and the Pyramids with Bronze Age Technology," in his *How to Build a Flying Saucer and Other Proposals in Speculative Engineering* (Prentice Hall, 1981)"

Pawlicki summarizes the question that archeologists have debated and attempted to explain for centuries and on which engineers have offered their opinions. Responding in his essay, Pawlicki offers some clear and plausible explanations. Having worked for several years in heavy earth construction, including the supervision of a site project in an industrial town, Pawlicki discusses various standard techniques used by the ancients. He explains that these methods, which prove both simple and economical, have been passed down in the trade through experience and oral tradition from one generation to the next, since time immemorial.

STONEHENGE

In respect to the construction of Stonehenge, Pawlicki addresses the challenge of lifting exceedingly massive lintels (the horizontal stones atop the columns). He explains that the Neolithic construction crews probably raised these stones to the top of the posts by a modification of the technique that they used to erect the vertical columns. Pawlicki states, "First the crew had to buttress the uprights with timbers and earthen fill.... When the lintel is brought to the base of the buttress on its boat [a wooden sled for moving large stones along timber rails], an H-frame is raised on stone pads on the other side of the arch. Lines are fastened to the stoneboat and thrown over the legs of the H-frame. The weight of a ballast box suspended by the lines keeps the H-frame upright. A chain gang mounts a scaffold and fills the ballast box with stones. If the distance over which the box will fall is measured carefully to equal the distance the lintel must rise, the H-frame will slowly rotate on its bottom legs, drawing the lintel up the ramp on the buttress until it comes to a gentle stop right above the pins receiving it."

Pawlicki continues by discussing the practical ways in which a Bronze Age crew could move large stones over great distances economically, including taking advantage of changes in elevations by lifting the stone only once to a high point. The crew then would have moved the stone the remainder of the distance by using gravity to slide it downhill.

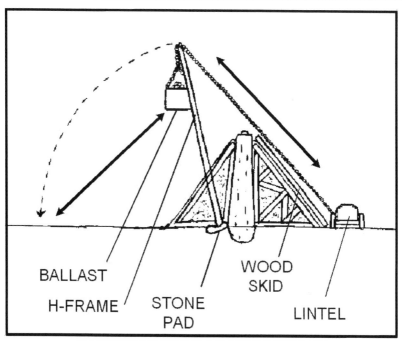

BALLAST

H-FRAME STONE PAD

WOOD SKID

LINTEL

RAISING LINTELS AT STONEHENGE

In respect to the Pyramids at Giza, Pawlicki suggests that workmen would not have used this kind of engineering in a competitive industry even though earthen ramps (such as the buttresses at Stonehenge) would have been plausible. In moving thousands of large stones, the earthen ramps would have deteriorated quickly under continuous and heavy use because earth flows under pressure. He asserts that the way a Bronze Age crew would have raised the stones to their level of placement likely would have involved building two wooden skidways that went up opposite sides of the pyramid. Then, this crew would have attached a rope to the stoneboat, run this line over two primitive pulleys mounted on the flat top of the incomplete pyramid, and thrown the rope to the other side. By tying a rock-filled ballast box to equal the weight of the stone being raised, the crew would have slid this box down the skids on the opposite side of the pyramid, thus drawing the structural stone slowly to the top.

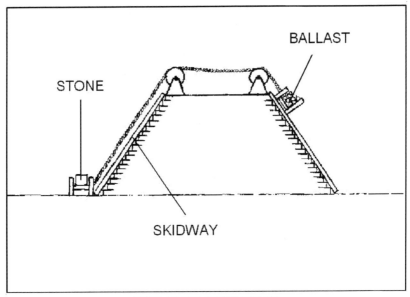

PYRAMID BUILDING

Addressing the matter of precision, Pawlicki continues by stating that apprentices would have dressed the surfaces of the stones already in place. The skilled crew then would have mounted the new stone atop long bags filled with sand while spreading a wet clay incline underneath the stone. By slowly emptying the sand bags, the stone would settle down onto the wet clay. The most difficult part of the operation would have entailed assistants quickly pulling out the empty bags from underneath the stone without losing one of their hands.

Meanwhile the skilled crew gently would guide the stone while slowly and completely squeezing the wet clay out from underneath. Given the slight incline of the clay platform, skilled stone-setters could slowly guide the new stone to its rest, an operation often achieving precision of within a millimeter. In conclusion, Pawlicki notes that it is economics rather than physics that lead modern stone-setters to adhere to standard tolerances of a quarter of an inch rather than a millimeter. In the twenty-first century CE, the time value of skilled stone-setters is much more expensive, relative to the cost of the same labor in ancient Egypt. In comparison to our modern methods, Bronze Age systems represented low technology/ high labor intensity work. At that time, labor was cheap. However, in respect to efficiency, we can hardly improve upon it today.

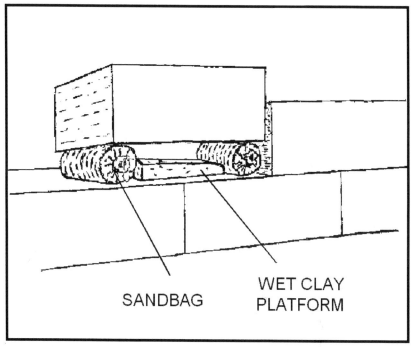

SANDBAG

WET CLAY PLATFORM

SETTING STONES ON THE PYRAMIDS

In the recent millennium, we often have built "modern" structures atop ancient pagan sites. In France and elsewhere, the Church of Rome purposely converted, or erected anew, many religious monuments over ancient temples. As a result, this conversion of space helped to facilitate the transfer of worship from a sea goddess to the Blessed Virgin Mary, who then may have assumed the additional name of "Star of the Sea." Such endeavors also aided in the transfer of the adoration of various sun gods to St. John the Baptist. Alternately, Charlemagne and other rulers took more extreme measures by destroying the

Saxon shrine of Heresburg, the center of mother goddess worship, and Irminsul, the sacred world tree of the Saxons.

Nevertheless, Christian Rome often built churches over ancient structures in order to assimilate pagan rituals rather than oppose the practitioners directly. The reconstructions served more than one purpose. For example, researchers tell us that a Celtic sun temple may have stood beneath the chapel at Lanleff, France. Some architectural historians have asserted that the Cisterian monks of St. Bernard replicated the former pagan purpose in the design of their own chapel.

St. Vincent de Paul founded the Lazarist order. In addition to the good works of charity for which the order is known, it maintains a site in the Languedoc named Notre-Dame de Marceille that is dedicated to the Black Virgin. Built over a pagan sacred place in the eleventh century, it remains a pilgrimage destination to this day. Along with many others, the Lazarist order participated in ceremonies marking the stages in the restoration and completion of the parish at Rennes-le-Chateau by its pastor, Father Francois Berenger Sauniere. In this village, the land owned by the Church sits above underground vaults developed a millennium earlier by the Cathars and Templars.

In his popular novel *The Da Vinci Code*, Dan Brown drew heavily from the stories surrounding of Father Sauniere and Rennes-le-Chateau. Likewise, the Church of Saint-Sulpice in Paris plays a pivotal role in Brown's novel. However, fewer people realize that the Paris Meridian brass Roseline that runs through the church and marks 17 January at sunrise actually honors the feast day of Saint Roseline who lived in the thirteenth-century.

Associated with Saint-Sulpice, we also find that a secret society named the Compagnie du Saint-Sacrement was formed in the seventeenth century. Encouraged covertly by King Louis XIII, the society worked openly with the Huguenots and became known as the "devout cabal." This company, which includes St. Vincent de Paul as a member, is noted for its work in caring for the impoverished of Paris. On a more political side, the company served as the foundation for those who built the city of Montreal in New France.

In contrast to the Sulpicians, the Jesuits, an order of Catholic priests founded by St. Ignatius Loyola, emerged as the new Papal militia in the Americas. Unfortunately for many religious and political interests, infighting between the Sulpicians and the Jesuits in Montreal and beyond hindered the growth of a unified New France.

Perhaps of greater importance to our quest, is the fact that the City of Montreal was founded and developed upon a more ancient city. The native name for this village was Hochelaga, possibly the French spelling of an Algonquian word for volcano, since it was claimed that a dormant volcano exists in the city. Based upon explorer Jacques Cartier's description from 1535 CE, the Native American settlement of Hochelaga was a planned village that had numerous streets laid out in a grid pattern with a central plaza. Ancient Hochelaga remains a district of the new city that was named by Cartier. The City of Montreal shares its name with a Templar castle in the Languedoc region of France. Hence, the name is a befitting tribute by the Compagnie du Saint-Sacrement, which desired to make Montreal the new Arcadia, where diversity, science and open-mindedness would be tolerated.

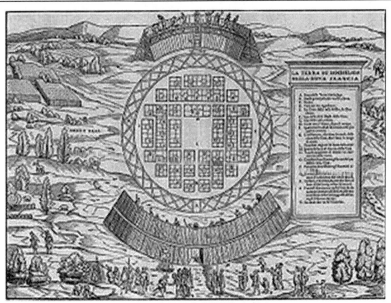

MAP OF HOCHELAGA

Chapter 4
THE MYSTERY BEGINS TO UNFOLD

From 1989 to 1992, I wrote my dissertation, *The Development Business Subcenters in Radial Monocentric Cities.* While doing my research, I discovered the Alaise alignments, a series of twenty-four paths radiating outward from a point located fifty miles northwest of Lake Geneva. These paths were identified by Xavier Guichard in the early twentieth century.

In recent years, I refueled my interest in the combinations of natural and human-made alignments after reading the books *The Holy Place: Saunière and the Decoding of the Mystery of Rennes-le-Château* by Henry Lincoln; *Genisis: the First Book of Revelations* by David Wood; *The Templars' Secret Island: The Knights, the Priest, and the Treasure* by Erling Haagensen and Henry Lincoln; and *Sacred Geometry: Philosophy and Practice* by Robert Lawlor. In their pages, I found that the propensity of humankind is to combine natural coincidences with Sacred Geometry in order to complete large and complex patterns upon the face of the earth. After purchasing the official map of the Langedoc region of France as recommended by Mr. Lincoln, I recreated the measurements and alignments that he found.

Born and raised in Michigan, I grew up in a real estate family. From them, I learned about local mounds and other Pre-European sites. Part of my father's family had emigrated from the Alaise region of Europe to America. Given his family background (along with a professional interest in all things related to real estate), my father passed along legends of how the early inhabitants of Europe established places and built structures that fit sets of geometric alignments. At that time, research was limited. In addition, most of oral tradition was treated as hearsay. Through the years, the notion of these alignments continued to hold my interest. However, after reading Henry Lincoln's *Sacred Places* a few years ago, I came to the conclusion that there may be much more to learn about these alignments that can be supported scientifically.

After studying the works of Lincoln, Wood, and Guichard, I began to wonder if similar alignments might exist on this continent as well. In my preliminary research, I found that others have attempted to make sense of the complex placement of mounds throughout the Midwestern United States. Working from a background in Urban Economics and a resulting familiarity with the geometry of place and planning throughout Western History, I learned that mathematics did not develop as the private domain of western culture. Given what we know about the lineage of geometry that Pythagoras learned at the Temple School of Giza in Egypt, evidence exists that our western knowledge of Sacred Geometry comes from the Vastu Shastra found in earlier Vedic texts from India. This book contains the mathematics used for sacred architecture. However, where Sacred Geometry developed originally remains a mystery, as this knowledge remains embedded in ancient structures throughout the world.

Therefore, I decided to delve into local Pre-European/Pre-Columbian culture within Michigan and Ohio. The obvious point of departure appeared in my mind as the collection of well-known mounds located on the former Hopewell farm near Chilicothe, Ohio, referred to collectively as Mound City. Though numerous students of these mounds debate the accuracy of the various survey maps drawn during the past century and a half, I chose to start with the survey map of North Fork Works created by Ephraim Squier and Edwin Davis in 1848. Given that Thomas Jefferson, William Burt, and other surveyors of early America had created accurate maps, I found no reason why any pair of at least halfway competent surveyors using nineteenth-century tools could not produce an accurate measure. Furthermore, I discovered that Squier and Davis had produced their map after they began the first major extraction of the site in 1845, two decades before any subsequent archeological digs.

Downloading a copy of the original map, I loaded it into a popular drawing/drafting program. This program provided me with the tools that I needed to measure and sketch rectangles, triangles, and circles. In playing with these tools and the map, I discovered a number of alignments at the Hopewell Mound City that produced geometric shapes of regular proportions and angles. The shapes included 30-60-90 and 20-70-90 right triangles, squares, rectangles, and parallel lines.

Coincidence? Perhaps. However, the regularity and multiplicity of these shapes encouraged me to contact my cousin, Robert Fritchie. Bob excelled in his profession of aerospace engineering and worked with renowned scientist Marcel Vogel (whom Bob mentioned in his preface to this book). A mentally disciplined person, Bob remains open-minded. In addition to his aerospace work, he has scientifically explored crystals, and the energy of sacred sites around the world.

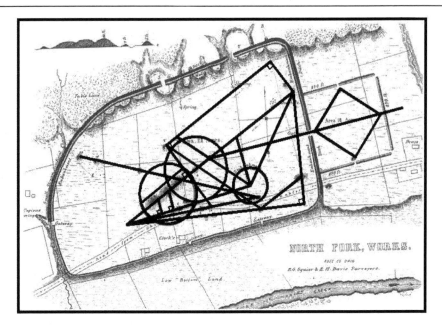

HOPEWELL MOUND CITY

With delight, I e-mailed my sketch to him. Cousin Bob (aka CB) responded to me (Cousin John, aka CJ) with the following missive.

Hi CJ,

VELLLLLY interesting. I do not believe in coincidences, so this to me is significant and indicative of something, but what?

If you ran a sight line from the least angle along the hypotenuse of the large triangle and the smaller triangle (the one to the lower right that shares the common right angle), it would describe a corridor or path. Where would that projection go? Think in terms of hundreds of miles, not yards.

Also, there may be another site with similar angular layouts. If so, I would not be surprised if the extend line of sight intersected at a third spot, indicative of something important. This could be associated with strong energy along ley lines, an energy vortex, or something altogether different.

In other structures around the world, pyramids and mounds point to something of greater consequence, sometimes a star system and sometimes a landmark.

Peace,
CB

Prompted by Bob's encouragement and my discovery of Google Earth, I looked intently at other ancient sites throughout southern Ohio. I discovered a number of interesting coincidences. Moreover, the generally accepted theory that geometric alignments served ancient cultures in both spiritual and practical matters hit me in a flash. Concurrent to my study of Hopewell, I had located a number of overlays online that marked the location of approximately 500 mounds discovered and explored by Professor Wilbert B. Hinsdale who taught at the University of Michigan during the early twentieth century.

Many in the field refer to Hinsdale as the father of Michigan archeology. Originally, Hinsdale was the dean and later the director of the Homeopathic Medical College at the University of Michigan. However, he has become better known to many for his seminal work in Michigan archeology. He published a number of books through the University of Michigan Press, including *Primitive Man in Michigan* (1925) and *The Archaeological Atlas of Michigan* (1931).

From local lore and oral traditions of Detroit, documented in the *Memorials of a Half Century* (1887) by Bela Hubbard, *A History of Detroit and Michigan* (1884) by Silas Farmer, and various other works, I recalled that the largest mound in the region had been the Great Mound of the Rouge. Ancient

37

habitants of the region established it as a burial and ceremonial mound at the mouth of the Rouge River at the point at which it flows into the Detroit River. This river, which is really a strait, forms the connecting channel between Lake St. Clair and Lake Erie. Before its demolition, which served to create space for the building of the Ford Motor Company Rouge facility in the 1920s, this mound stood forty feet tall, two hundred feet wide, and four hundred feet long (i.e., longer than a football field and as tall as a four-story building).

The Great Mound of the Rouge stood 200 English furlong miles north of the Hopewell mounds. By measurement against the rotational pole of the Earth, the Rouge Mound stood a few miles off center of a point due north of Hopewell. I asked myself the question, "Could the ancient culture that built these mounds originally have used measurement tools of great precision?"

Because the Hopewell civilization flourished in the Midwest between 500 BCE and 1300 CE, it would have been possible for the culture to have been introduced to the Chinese magnetic compass that existed at that time. In addition, geologists have approximated and mapped the drift of the magnetic north pole over the course of the past two millennia. Using these measurements on a Google Earth map, it is possible to track the movement of the magnetic pole between 150 CE and 1200 CE, back and forth across the path of the rotational pole. It appears that the magnetic line reached its easternmost point around 350 CE and its westernmost point around 1200 CE. The Great Mound of the Rouge would have appeared due north, magnetically, about 150 CE and again in 1000 CE.

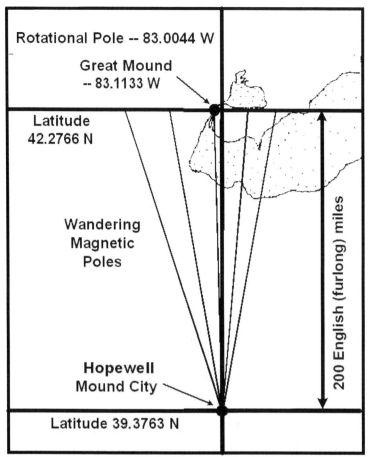

MOUND CITY AND THE GREAT MOUND OF THE ROUGE

In drawing this map, I noticed that the Rouge Mound lay slightly north of 42 degrees north of the equator. Recalling that the baseline of the Rennes-le-Chateau alignments identified by Henry Lincoln and David Woods was described as 42 degrees, 55 minutes, and 39 seconds north of the equator, I wondered if this coincidence might bear fruit in exploration. Therefore, I plotted the 42° 55' 39" North parallel around the globe. For convenience, we will refer to this parallel as the Rennes-le-Chateau parallel. Curiously, this line touched the site of the ancient gateway to the Silk Road located in the city of Urumqui,

China,[10] passed through the Langedoc region of France, and extended beyond Michigan to the south shore of Wizard Island in Crater Lake that is located in Oregon,[11] located 105 miles due north of Mount Shasta in northern California. I recognized the significance that these sites hold in multiple realms of thought.

Returning my focus to Michigan, I noticed that this line of latitude passes through two large concentrations of mounds. The first group lies due north of the Great Mound of the Rouge[12] in Macomb County at the end of Mound Road. The second group lies north of Lansing, Michigan, in Clinton County.[13] Dr. Hinsdale and other archeologists noted that this second locale contains the largest concentration of mounds in Michigan. Drawing a straight line from this point in Clinton County to the Rouge Mound completes a 30-60-90 degree triangle with the short side connecting the Clinton and Rouge mound sites.

Curious? Perhaps. However, I am not one to be easily convinced that these observations are anything more than coincidence, for as Tweedle Dee said in Lewis Carroll's book *Alice in Wonderland*, "The oysters were curious, too, weren't they?" I did notice that there are two other mound clusters along a longitude that lies 90 degrees west of the origin point of the Alaise alignments. For convenience, let us refer to this longitudinal line as the Alaise meridian offset.

---

[10] (42° 55' 56" N at 87° 34' 58" E)
[11] (42° 55' 39" N at 122° 08' 52" W)
[12] (aka Delray Mound, 42° 16' 39" N at 83° 06' 42" W)
[13] (circa 42° 55' 39" N and 84° 37' 50" W)

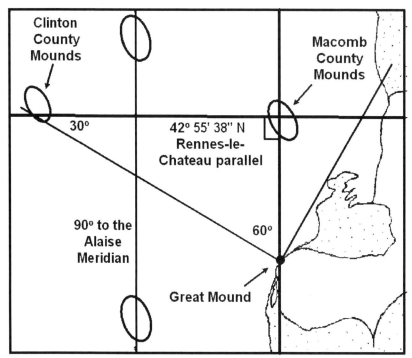

EASTERN MICHIGAN MOUND GROUPS

Zooming outward, we can appreciate the relative locations of these few points of interest. Also, let us note that the Rennes-le-Chateau parallel passes through another area containing a series of mounds. This area is located just south of the city of Grand Rapids. The parallel continues westward along the south side of Milwaukee, Wisconsin, through the community of West Alis (any possible connection to the name Alaise?).

Extending the hypotenuse from the Clinton group through the site of the Rouge Mound takes us "spot on" to the Central Business District of Cleveland, Ohio. Finally, extending a line from the Hopewell and Henneberger Mounds, north by northeast through Cleveland creates another 30-60-90 degree right triangle.

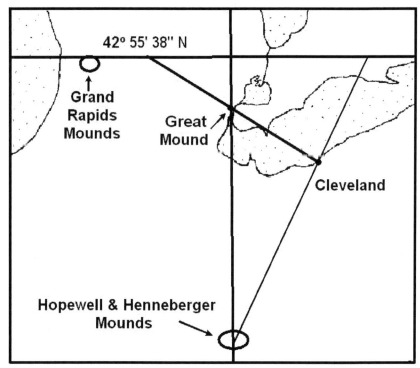

42° 55' 38" N

Grand
Rapids
Mounds

Great
Mound

Cleveland

Hopewell & Henneberger
Mounds

MICHIGAN AND OHIO OVERVIEW

By extending the Alaise offset line due south through the center
of the lower peninsula of Michigan and southwards, we find
that this line passes along the outskirts of the city of Atlanta,
Georgia.[14] I then extended this longitudinal line to the South
Pole. From the pole, I drew lines north by northwest and north
by northeast to the visible end-points along the to the Rennes-
le-Chateau parallel. From this exercise, I discovered two new
occurrences of interest. Drawing a line between the two visible
end points of this parallel produced a line that passed west to
east through the city of Atlanta, Georgia. This interested me
mildly. However, the second occurrence would prove to be of
greater significance. The right-hand hypotenuse of this pair of
right triangles passed through Machu Picchu, the lost Incan city

---

[14] I call attention to this anomaly because David Wood points to the location of the site of
Atlantis, (42° 55'18" N at 26° 06' 07" W).

42

that was located high in the Andes[15] in Peru. We will return to Machu Picchu as a key piece in a larger puzzle.

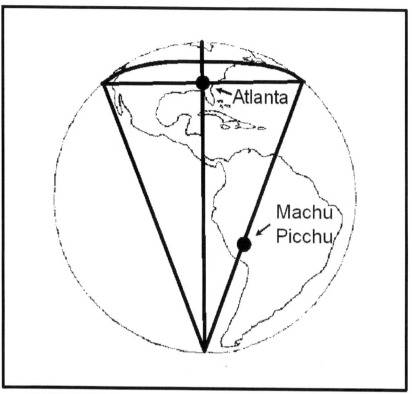

CONNECTIONS TO ATLANTA AND MACHU PICCHU

Ancient cultures often drew lines upon the earth and placed structures at points along these lines to reflect groupings of stars and planets appearing in the night sky. However, the drawing of constellations remains culturally subjective, though much attention has been given to the pattern that western culture refers to as the constellation Orion. Working within the context of Sacred Geometry, I realized that one can derive the stylized shape of Orion from a simple set of geometric forms. We will return to this discussion later in our exploration.

---

[15] (13° 09' 51" S at 72° 32' 44" W)

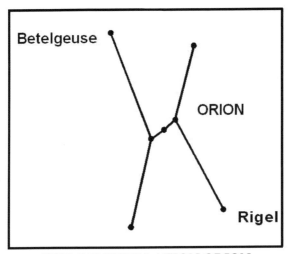

THE CONSTELLATION ORION

Following my cousin Bob's suggestion, I began to explore more distant sites. Early in our discussions, he suggested that I explore the natural energy vortices located in the area around Sedona, Arizona. Finding sites-of-interest maps at Sedona's online visitor's center, I paused to appreciate the beauty of the area in the many available photographs. I then took up the task of pinpointing the major vortices by using Google Earth software. I identified four sites.

BOYNTON CANYON

After pasting the screen shot of the Sedona Vortices into my drawing program, I transferred my measurements from Google Earth into my program calculations. The four principle points include: the Boynton Canyon Vortex,[16] the Airport Mesa Vortex,[17] the Cathedral/Red Rock Vortex,[18] and the Bell Rock Vortex.[19] From this data, I sketched the following set of alignments and their measures.

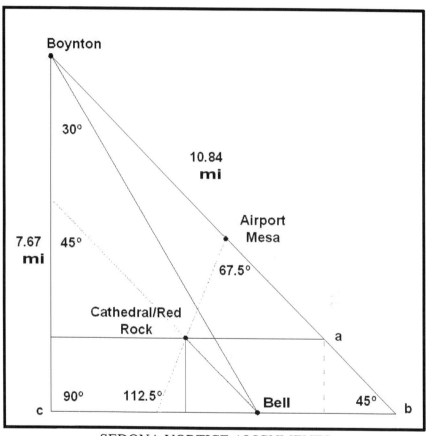

SEDONA VORTICE ALIGNMENTS

[16] (34° 54' 44" N at 111° 50' 55" W)

[17] (34° 51' 20" N at 111° 46' 47" W)

[18] (34° 49' 26"N at 111° 47' 48" W)

[19] (34° 48' 02" N at 111° 46' 03" W)

In the Sedona drawing, I established the height and the base of the geometry. Next, I sketched a line from the Boynton Canyon vortex to point c and then from point c through the Bell vortex to point b. Adding the hypotenuse from Boynton to Bell, I discovered a 30-60-90 triangle. I then drew another hypotenuse from Bell through the Cathedral/Red Rock site and discovered that this line created a 45-45-90 triangle.

Finally, I extended a line from Boynton through Airport Mesa and continued this line until it intersected the base at intercept b, I found that this path paralleled the Bell-Cathedral/Red Rock line and, consequently, produced another 45-45-90 triangle. Perhaps some correlation exists between natural energy vortices and geometry in a form that ancient inhabitants with primitive tools could have discovered. "Curiouser and curiouser," as Lewis Carroll's Alice would say.

As a side note: Frank Lloyd Wright, the master of geometric architectural design, built his Taliesin West studio near Scottsdale, Arizona, precisely ninety miles due south of the Boynton Canyon Vortex. Taliesin West served Wright as his winter home and school in the desert from 1937 until his death in 1959 at the age of ninety-one.

Chapter 5
THE ALAISE ALIGNMENTS

During the research for my dissertation, I came across the Alaise alignments recorded by Xavier Guichard during the 1920s.

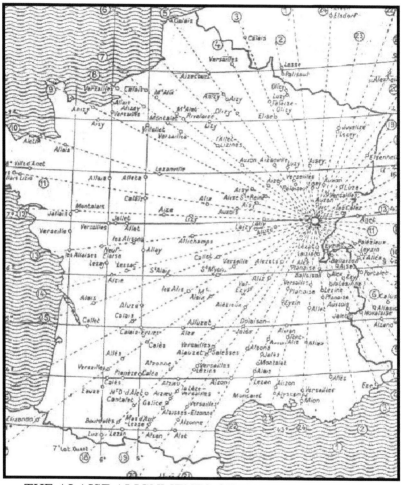

THE ALAISE ALIGNMENTS OF XAVIER GUICHARD

The Alaise alignments extend radially outward from the area of a town in France known as Alaise. Xavier Guichard discovered a set of twenty-four alignments that extend from this point. He claimed that the radii pass through sites associated with ancient wells and sacred places, all bearing names derived from Alaise (e.g., Alais, Calais, and Versailles). For many years, I held this fact as an intellectual amusement--that is, until I started this current project.

Some writers, such a David Wood, have suggested that the place name of Alaise connects to a transplanted group that continued to follow the Egyptian religion of Isis and named the site as *a la Isis*. He and other authors suggest that the name Paris is derived from *Par-Isis*, in relation to an ancient temple of Isis (at Versailles). Also, the name *Champs-Elysées* literally translates as *Elysian-fields*. Though perhaps a bit speculative, I find these assertions plausible and demanding of further research.

Of course, the naming of the patterns that we find remains secondary to the existence of the patterns identified. David Wood and other writers cover the name speculations thoroughly. Therefore, in order to avoid a duplication of effort, I have chosen to focus upon the location and patterns themselves, as well as their connections to other geometric sites around the world.

Though a number of rises or clearings are in the neighborhood of the village of Alaise, I began with the coordinates 47° 00' 50" N at 5° 58' 26" E as the center point. In the process of replicating Guimard's work, I found that the twenty-four lines intersect one another in an area measuring a diameter of six-miles.

While searching through older geopolitical maps of Europe, I found one entitled *The Rise of the Frankish Empire*. In this map, the cartographer sketched and coded the various kingdoms that eventually composed the Frankish Empire, a territory that reached its peak during the first millennium CE. On the map in front of me, I saw the names of the kingdoms that created the Merovingian bloodline as well as the location of geometrically connected sites of the Cathar region of the Septimania where the 42° 55' 39" N Rennes-le-Chateau parallel crosses the old Paris (Roseline) Meridian.

The Merovingian line was founded by Merowig (numerous pronunciations). The most famous ruler descended from this line was Clovis (Louis) who expanded the realm greatly between 481 and 511 CE. The Merovingian line originated through the merger of the principal female line of Septimania to the principal male line of the Salian (coastal dwelling) Franks.

The center point of the Alaise alignments is located in the middle of this former empire in the north of Burgundy. Out of curiousity, I transplanted and scaled the Alaise drawings that I had made previously and laid them over this older map. I added the longitudinal line that I labeled as the Alaise Meridian.[20] Because a succession of prime meridians has dominated maps of Europe over the centuries, I also included the meridians that pass through Paris,[21] Greenwich[22] and Stonehenge.[23] At various times in the past, all four of these meridians may have served as astronomical coordinates for spiritual, agricultural, and other purposes.

---

[20] (5° 58' 26" E)
[21] (2° 20' 14" E)
[22] (0° 00' 00")
[23] (1° 49' 34" W)

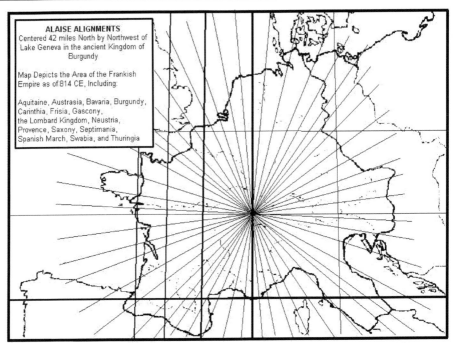

ALAISE ALIGNMENTS
Centered 42 miles North by Northwest of
Lake Geneva in the ancient Kingdom of
Burgundy

Map Depicts the Area of the Frankish
Empire as of 814 CE, Including:

Aquitaine, Austrasia, Bavaria, Burgundy,
Carinthia, Frisia, Gascony,
the Lombard Kingdom, Neustria,
Provence, Saxony, Septimania,
Spanish March, Swabia, and Thuringia

FRANKISH EMPIRE WITH SUPERIMPOSED MERIDIANS

Chapter 6
ON THE SHOULDERS OF OTHERS

While Googling for mounds, alignments, and other pertinent objects, I came across a drawing of the Great Lakes Biome prepared by Peter Champoux, co-author of *Gaia Matrix: Arkhom & the Geometries of Destiny in the North American Landscape*. What struck me was the location of three of the five corners of the pentagon and pentangle. These corners are located at the end-points of three of the five Great Lakes. Furthermore, the center point of the drawing is located at Sault Saint Marie at the Michigan-Ontario border. I thought that Mr. Champoux had done a wonderful job, though it appeared that he had worked with a relatively small drawing and that his sketch may not have accounted accurately for the slight curvature of the Earth.

The requirement of scientific relicability demands that another researcher should be able to start with the same assumptions and the same data and be able to replicate the results. Also, given the present widespread availability of Google Earth, I decided that I would push for even greater precision in the measurement and sketching of the Biome diagram.

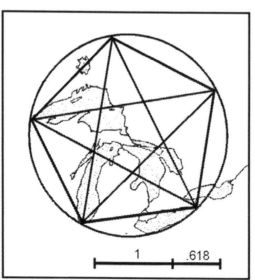

THE GREAT LAKES BIOME—PETER CHAMPOUX 2002

51

As I searched for the precise coordinates of the five corner points of the pentagon, a couple of light bulbs lit up in my brain. I discovered that the southeast corner at the Niagara River existed at 42° 55′ 39″N, the Rennes-le-Chateau parallel. Furthermore, the city center of Detroit appeared to be located at the midpoint of the southern base of the pentagon. Being familiar with the existence of a number of former ancient burial/ceremonial sites and markers in this part of town, I began to wonder if there was any special significance to this coincidence.

Chapter 7
QUESTIONS ARISE AS THE MYSTERY FORMS

As I measured the slight leftward offset of the pentagon, another concern materialized. Does one simply spin the Sacred Geometry to make it fit or is there some other underlying logic that determines the positioning of this artwork? The apparent natural phenomenon includes a peninsula that looks like a mitten. In Michigan, we carry our map in our hands. When we need a map, we simply point to the location of various cities, towns, etc. on our palms, fingers, and thumbs. It's a Michigan thing.

I asked myself, "Why is the Great Lakes Biome offset by thirteen degrees in respect to the rotational-pole?" Before proceeding any further in my quest, I needed to make sense of this inherent offset in order to convince myself that the Champoux drawing was more than just a pretty picture. The center point at the Soo (Sault Saint Marie) constitutes an obvious anchor point in his drawing. However, where is the location of that precise point? To answer this question, I turned to Michigan history. I found that the prime meridian for measuring both Michigan and Ohio townships was first marked in the ground in October, 1815 by Benjamin Hough. In June, 1840, American inventor/surveyor William A. Burt carried out an important assignment for the Federal government and for Michigan. He extended the principal meridian[24] across the Straits of Mackinac and onward to the south shore of Lake Superior.

Burt invented the solar compass and served as the supervisor in the construction of the original set of ship locks between Lake Superior and Lake Huron that opened in May, 1855. The locks

---

[24] (84° 22' 24" W)

bypass the rapids of the St. Mary's River where the water falls twenty-one feet from Lake Superior.

In addition, Burt establlshicd tho meridian for the purpose of the initial measurement of townships in Michigan and Uniu. Tlit aberrations of the magnetic needle proved such a problem that Burt devised his famous solar compass as a means to obtain accurate township lines. His solar compass was highly successful and was eventually adopted by the U.S. Federal government for all of its surveys. Though the marker of the Michigan meridian/baseline marker sets just northeast of Jackson, Michigan, the meridian line starts at a point along the St. Mary's River at the Soo.

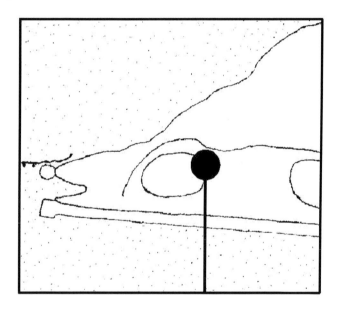

CENTER POINT AT THE SOO

The northernmost point in the area of the Soo sits along the St. Mary's River. Burt had the task of extending the existing meridian from downstate. My task was to find the most probable point used by the ancient inhabitants to cross the river and to mark the center of the biome geometry. As a result, I

54

fixed the center point at what may have served as the logical crossing point along the river. This gathering place to meet others and to safely cross above the rapids is located four-tenths of a mile east of Burt's mark.

Over the past millennia, the rapids of the St. Mary's River may have shifted and changed in length. However, for practical reasons that hold to this day, it is likely that early travelers would have crossed at the narrows of the river above the rapids. Following this logic, I selected a center point located at 84° 21' 53" W on the Canadian side of the straits.

THE SOO LOCKS—ORIGINAL

THE SOO LOCKS TODAY

Chapter 8
STEPPING OFF INTO SPACE

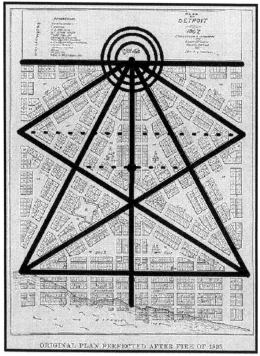

GEOMETRIC PLAN OF CENTRAL DETROIT, 1805

My avid interest in the history of Old Detroit led me to explore a number of potential points that may form the precise midpoint along the pentagon base. The Great Mound of the Rouge presented itself as an early candidate. Also, the records of the early Jesuit missionaries document their finding and subsequent destruction of a totem to the god Manitou. The stone carving of this deity stood near the shoreline of the Detroit River. Until the riverfront was extended outward through a series of landfills in the nineteenth century, the shoreline sat further back along what is now Jefferson Avenue. An early French legend tells us that, after the missionaries destroyed the totem, they loaded the remaining chunk of black stone into a canoe and dumped it into the deep water near White Swan Island (now Belle Isle, Detroit's island park). The exact location of the site at which the totem stood remains debatable. However, the Catholic Church traditionally has co-opted pagan spiritual sites for various reasons (e.g. the Vatican Basilica stands upon such a site in Rome). The first Catholic cathedral in Detroit, that later became Saints Peter and Paul Jesuit Church adjacent to the University of Detroit Mercy Law School, may have been this site.

Curiosity prompted me to ask where the path from the Soo through Detroit would lead me. Using the ruler tool in Google Earth, I extended a couple of lines down through South America. After checking and rechecking the general locations of the pass-through points in Detroit, I locked down the ruler line and went exploring with the help of the Google Earth Geographic Web. The path that went from the Soo through downtown Detroit, at what was most likely an ancient crossing point to Canada, took me into the Peruvian Andes. More precisely, it took me to the sacred, abandoned city of Machu Picchu. (An alternate path, passing through the Rouge Mound, led to a point about halfway between the Nazca Glyphs and Machu Picchu.) I decided to lock the southern end of the ruler line to the outcropping of rock that stands at the south end of the plaza in Machu Picchu and then return to Michigan to check my measurements.

THE LOST INCAN CITY OF MACHU PICCHU

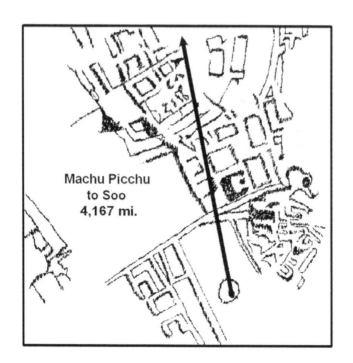

Machu Picchu
to Soo
4,167 mi.

ALIGNMENT TO THE LARGE OUTCROPPING

I selected this outcropping in Machu Picchu[25] as the end point of the trajectory from the Soo.

Returning north to Detroit, I found that the Soo to Machu Picchu alignment passed just east of the Renaissance Center complex (General Motors World Headquarters) that is south of Jefferson Avenue. As this location would not have existed before the nineteenth-century landfill, I proceeded to look at sites along Jefferson Avenue.

APPROXIMATE FORMER LOCATION
OF THE MANITOU TOTEM

Looking slightly north along the north side of Jefferson Avenue, I found that the Soo to Machu Picchu alignment passes through the bell tower and sacristy of Saints Peter and Paul Jesuit Church.[26] Further along this route, the alignment passes along the front steps of Saint Mary's Church.[27] In addition, this line passes within .75 miles of the former site of a mound that once stood along Chene Street. A few miles north of the area shown

---

[25] (13° 09′ 51″ S at 72° 32′ 44″ W)
[26] (42° 19′ 54″ N at 83° 02′ 17″ W)
[27] (42° 20′ 09″ N at 83° 02′ 21″ W)

60

in the picture, the alignment passes within .5 miles of the former location of a group of mounds north of East Euclid Street. This location is on the industrial property of the Great Lakes Smelting Company,[28] and a city block east of St. Florian's Church in Hamtramck.[29] Also, one can find a number of sites further north of these guide points, including a number of earthwork sites near Unionville, Michigan,[30] near the south shore of Saginaw Bay. Professor Hinsdale listed these sites in his exploration of Michigan mounds during the early twentieth century.

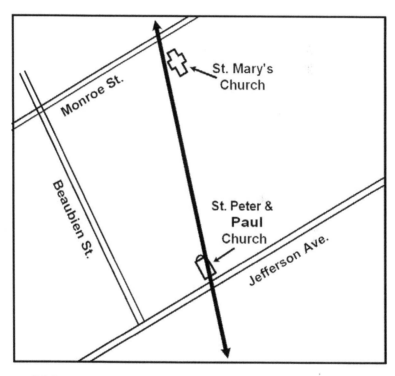

SOO – MACHU PICCHU LINE THROUGH DETROIT

For comparison, using an alternate center point at the Soo, located at the William Burt marker in the park on the mainland

---

[28] (42° 23′ 03″ N at 83° 03′ 49″ W)

[29] (42° 23′ 38″ N at 83° 03′ 29″ W)

[30] (43° 39′ 14″ N at 83° 27′ 57″ W)

at precisely 84° 22′ 24″ W, shifts the Detroit point six-tenths of a mile westward to the foot of Washington Boulevard at Cobo Hall.[31] Conversely, shifting the center point of the Soo eastward to the middle of the large island in the area of the rapids[32] would push the Detroit midpoint six-tenths of a mile eastward to the foot of St. Aubin Street.

Increasingly convinced that points of significance existed along the middle route, I chose to anchor the midpoint of the base of the pentagon at Saints Peter and Paul Jesuit Church because it sits on the alignment within yards of the original shoreline.[33]
My next task required integrating the geometry back to the core geometry from which Peter Champoux's diagram could be derived. In order to generate the length of *phi* (x * 1.618...) necessary to replicate Champoux's pentagon, pentangle, and circle, I needed to start with a series of interlocking circles. Into these circles, I would insert the Vesica Piscis (a straight line that passes through the overlap of two circles). This would allow me to generate the additional shapes that lead to the determination of the length *phi* that forms the sides of the pentagon of the Great Lakes Biome diagram.

The selected center point at the Soo constitutes the center of the upper circle.[34] With a bit of math, some help from my cousin Bob the engineer, and some old-fashioned trial and error using the ruler tool in Google Earth, I established the radius of the first circle. Since the circles must overlap to develop the Vesica Piscis, the center point of subsequent circles must be of the same diameter and must set upon the circumference of the preceding circle.

---

[31] (42° 19′ 39″ N at 83° 02′ 54″ W)
[32] (46° 30′ 35″ N at 84° 21′ 05″ W)
[33] (42° 19′ 54″ N at 83° 0 2′ 17″ W)
[34] (46° 30′ 49″ N at 84° 21′ 53″ W)

Therefore, let us establish the center point of the middle circle at a point in rural Michigan, slightly north of the AuSable River and Lumberman's Monument State Park, about .4 miles south/southwest of the junction of East M-72 and North M-65. The coordinates of this center point are 44° 38′ 45″ N at 83° 44′ 53″ W.

The third center point struck me as unusual because the geometric pattern of the constellation Orion can be stylized from Sacred Geometry of the Great Lakes Biome. We locate this third point[35] 3.5 miles due east of Lake Orion in Orion Township in a wooded area northeast of the intersection of Stony Creek and Lake George Roads. I continued to research the origin of the location name, Orion.

---

[35] (42° 46′ 27″ N at 83° 10′ 10″ W)

Chapter 9
DERIVING THE GREAT LAKES BIOME DIAGRAM

We are ready to recreate the Great Lakes Biome diagram using Google Earth. First, we have located and marked the three center points of the interlocking circles as well as the midpoint of the baseline of the pentagon. In my experience of using Google Earth, I have found that the ruler tool compensates for the curvature of the earth better than the "add path" tool. Therefore, I hope that I have achieved greater accuracy by locating the path with the ruler, locking it down, and then drawing a line or line segments over it. Only after I am satisfied with the line do I turn off the ruler.

THE TOUR BEGINS

The following section represents a guided tour through a cyber-museum, with me serving as your tour guide. Let us begin. As we walk through this maze of drawings, we will explore points of interest that you may wish to explore further. Also, I will provide and describe easy-to-locate sign posts in case you wish to replicate these works in finer, interactive detail. Let's have some fun exploring these curious alignments.

For visual contrast, I have redrawn the screen view of the Great Lakes and other regions of the world as line images. In the first frame, we view the primary center points that that we will use to construct the Great Lakes Biome drawing.

The bottom dot represents the Detroit midpoint of what will become the base of the primary pentagon in our final drawing. The three dots above Detroit represent the center points of our first three circles as described previously. The first dot marks the location of the lower circle center near Lake Orion, Michigan. The topmost dot marks the crossing point at the Soo.

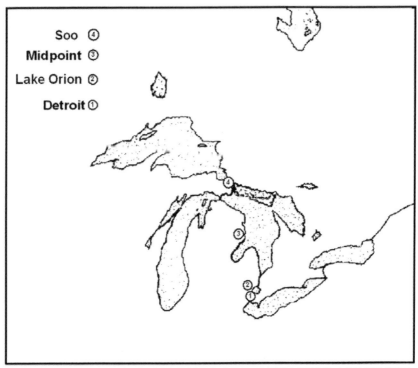

THE THREE CIRCLE CENTERS AND DETROIT BASE POINT

To provide a larger frame of reference as we complete our image and look beyond the Great Lakes Biome, let us insert the Michigan-Ohio meridian. Also, let us add the Rennes-le-Chateau parallel represented by a horizontal line. This latitude line passes through the geometry of Rennes-le-Chateau in France. (Note: As we add each new feature, we will highlight the feature in the initial rendering and then reduce its thickness or size in subsequent images. Hopefully, this technique will maintain intelligibility as the sketches grow more complex).

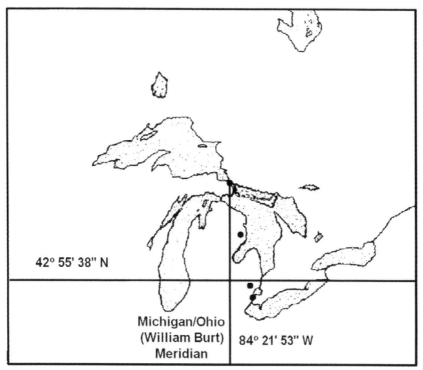

42° 55' 38" N

Michigan/Ohio
(William Burt)
Meridian

84° 21' 53" W

MICHIGAN-OHIO MERIDIAN &
RENNES-LE-CHATEAU ALIGNMENT

Next, we draw the straight path that extends from the Soo in Northern Michigan to Machu Picchu in Peru. Since the out-cropping at the southern end of the plaza in Machu Picchu lies 4,167 miles south of the Soo and 3,871 miles south of the median point of the base line in Detroit, Google Earth or a traditional globe may prove to be a more desirable medium than a flat map.

As we draw this line southward from the Soo, we pass through the other three center points in Michigan before travelling through the tip of Essex County, Ontario—the only part of Canada located south of the United States—and across Lake Erie into Ohio. Passing through the United States, we leave land at Hilton Head Island in South Carolina and head out to sea. As we continue over the Atlantic Ocean, we pass about fifteen miles from the Bimini Road that lies under the water between Miami, Florida, and the Bahama Islands.

Bimini Road is an underwater rock formation near North Bimini Island in the Bahamas. The Road consists of a linear "path" that is half-mile long composed of roughly rectangular limestone blocks. Since the discovery of the Road in 1968, investigators have found two additional "pavement-like" features that lie parallel to and shoreward of the Bimini Wall. As many observers have labeled it "The Road to Atlantis," the origin and use of the Bimini Road remains a topic of dispute.

Continuing southward, we pass over Cuba, Jamaica, and Columbia before reaching Peru. If you are using Google Earth or a similar program to follow along, you may want to turn on the terrain feature and adjust the horizon as we approach Machu Picchu. One can appreciate the grandeur of the Andes mountain range from this perspective. If we follow the river valley southward from Quillabamba, Peru, and travel far into the mountains, we pass a point where three rivers meet. Then we continue until the river turns east and is joined by another tributary. From this juncture, we proceed eastward about two miles upstream. At this point, if we ascend the mountain to the east for a third of a mile at a forty-five degree angle, we find ourselves atop the main plaza of Machu Picchu.[36]

Often referred to as "The Lost City of the Incas," Machu Picchu remains one of the most familiar symbols of the Incan Empire. The Incas started to build the city upon the site of a more ancient holy retreat around 1430 CE. A hundred years later at the time of the Spanish Conquest, the civilization abandoned it as an official site for Inca rulers. Machu Picchu remained intact, but it was unknown to the world at large for 500 years. Finally,

---

[36] (13° 09′ 49″ N at 72° 32′ 46″ W)

American historian Hiram Bingham brought the ruins to international attention in 1911. After decades of study and restoration, Machu Picchu was declared a UNESCO World Heritage Site in 1983.

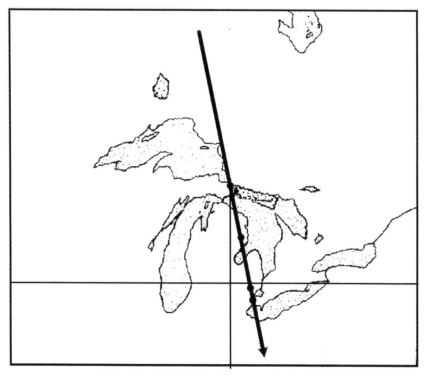

SOO-MACHU PICCHU ALIGNMENT

As I researched this site, the question arose in my mind as to why the region of the Great Lakes Biome would have a connection to Machu Picchu in the Peruvian Andes. The answer should appear simple to anyone interested in mineral deposits around the globe.

Of the four largest known deposits of copper in the world, two are connected by the Soo-Machu Picchu alignment. The south shore of Lake Superior, Isle Royale, and the region of Canada north of the lake have been mined since antiquity. Evidence exists that a culture worked these mines 4,500 years ago. The main shaft developed by the company that eventually would emerge as the Minnesota Mining and Manufacturing Company (3M) took advantage of an extensively deep dig left by an unknown Neolithic culture.

The second copper deposit appears in the Peruvian Andes at the opposite end of the Soo-Machu Picchu alignment and southward to an even more ancient site at Lake Titicaca. These deposits have been mined since an earlier millenium. Through geological survey maps, we find that both areas have held substantial deposits of gold and silver as well as an abundance of copper. Therefore, the simple but practical answer to the question of why this alignment was established may be answered in one word—wealth.

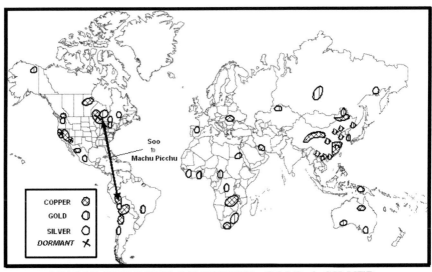

MAJOR DEPOSITS OF COPPER, GOLD & SILVER

Chapter 10
THE CIRCLES OF SACRED GEOMETRY

Given the preceding explanation for the offset of thirteen degrees to the geometry that overlays the Great Lakes Biome, let us proceed to derive the pentagon and pentangle rendered by Peter Champoux. We begin by adding five circles. Following the practice of Sacred Geometry, let us insert the middle circle in mid-Michigan. From the measurements derived, the radius of each of the five circles equals 132.28 miles. Because of the placement of the other two circle-center markers along the Soo-Machu Picchu alignment, the circumference of this first circle will pass through each of these points.

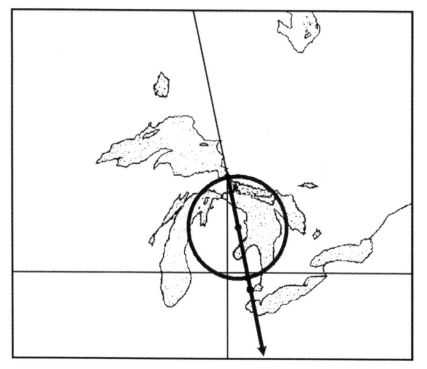

THE FIRST CIRCLE

We start by extending the first radius eastward into Lake Huron and then rotate the line clockwise. As it passes across the

71

Thumb of Michigan, the end of the radius passes within two miles of a series of ancient earthwork forts described by Hinsdale. These are located in northern Macomb County[37] due north of the Detroit midpoint.

After traversing the Orion center point, we swing the line upward through Clinton County, the location that Hinsdale cited as containing the greatest concentration of mounds in the state. There, we pass through the midst of a cluster of mounds.[38] Onward through the west side of the state, we come within one mile of a group of six mounds in Kent County.[39]

Continuing further north, we then pass through a mound group located in southern Newaygo County.[40] Further north, we pass through the midst of numerous clusters of mounds spread through northern Newaygo, Oceano, Mason, and Lake Counties,[41] before heading out and over Lake Michigan up toward the Soo. Finally, after passing over remote areas of Ontario, we return to our starting point.

Next on our journey, we head to the Soo locks to add the upper circle. We center this circle at the top of the Michigan-Ohio Meridian.

---

[37] (42° 50′ 31″ N at 82° 59′ 59″ W)
[38] (42° 55′ 18″ N at 84° 54′ 37″ W)
[39] (43° 06′ 43″ N at 85° 22′ 17″ W)
[40] (43° 21′ 51″ N at 85° 43′ 34″ W)
[41] in the area of 43° 49′ 05″ N at 86° 09′ 21″ W

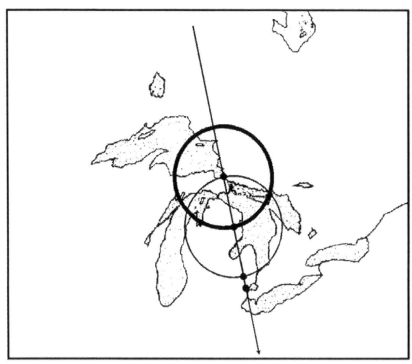

THE SECOND CIRCLE

Let us extend our radius to the east once again. Swinging our line clockwise, we pass over the north end of Lake Huron and head inland, passing through the center point of our first circle. Continuing onward through the western side of the peninsula, we pass through the resort region of Grand Traverse. Proceeding over the wine country of the Leelanau peninsula, we head out and over Lake Michigan and pass over South Manitou Island.[42] Leelanau often is referred to as the "little finger" of the mitten-shaped Lower Peninsula. Sleeping Bear Dunes National Lakeshore lines the west side of this peninsula. The Grand Traverse Band of Ottawa and Chippewa Native Americans inhabit the Leelanau peninsula in the vicinity of Peshawbestown.

---

[42] (45° 02' 07" N at 86° 06' 38" W)

Leelanau was named after Jane Johnston Schoolcraft, nineteenth-century author of Objiwa and Scots-Irish descent who wrote under the pen name Leelinau. The wife of territorial Indian agent Henry Rowe Schoolcraft, she has been recognized as the first Native American writer of literature. Schoolcraft was the first known Indian woman writer, the first known Indian poet, the first known poet to write in a Native American language, and the first known American Indian to write out traditional Indian stories. What little we know about pre-European culture in Michigan comes through the writings of Schoolcraft and a few other Native American authors.

Most of the sites of Michigan mounds appear in the bottom half of the Lower Peninsula. This may be due to the climate line that traverses the peninsula from Ludington on the west coast to the Saginaw Bay on the east coast. This abrupt transition in climate marks the limit of the southern part of the peninsula that enjoys a longer growing season. The most notable change that one encounters when heading north is the increased proportion of coniferous (pine) trees. In contrast, the major river systems and water sheds with their resulting high-quality soil predominate throughout the southern part of the state.

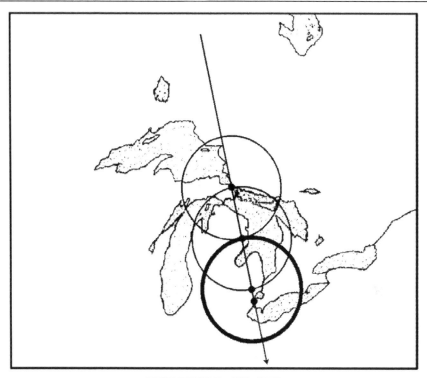

THE THIRD CIRCLE

We continue with the addition of the third circle centered near Lake Orion. Again, we extend the 132.28 mile-long radius eastward into Ontario. Rotating the radius clockwise, we pass through the southern side of Ontario and across Lake Erie. After passing south of Cleveland, we enter a region of Ohio that formed the expansive bed of a prehistoric lake. This region of fertile soil that extends westward across the state generally lacks Pre-Columbian mound and earthwork sites. The vast majority of the Ohio sites are found in the southern region of the state.

As we swing northward into Michigan, we encounter a proliferation of mounds once again. At the bottom of the peninsula, we pass among numerous mound groupings and earthworks in St. Joseph County.[43] Continuing our exploration, we pass again through the region of mound clusters that is spread through Allegan, Van Buren, and Kalamazoo counties.[44] Progressing northward toward Grand Rapids, we pass within one mile west of the grouping of seven mounds located in Grandville, Michigan.[45] As we enter Grand Rapids, we draw our circle through the neighborhood that includes the Converse mound group, the Norton mounds, the Hopewell mounds, and a number of other mounds and earthworks clustered within an area measuring six miles in diameter.[46]

Further north, we pass within two miles of what Hinsdale recorded as an unknown number of mounds in Mecosta County.[47] Next, we encounter a group of mounds and earthworks, located a few miles from our pen point in Osceola County[48] before proceeding into the region of the Lower Peninsula that lies above the climate line.

The measurement of the large Great Lakes pentangle within the outer pentagon requires the determination of a relative length *phi* in relation to the length of the sides of the pentagon. In order to determine this and other *phi* values, we need to generate the necessary square and resulting rectangle from which we can derive the values of *phi*. In order to complete this task, we need to add two additional circles that connect tangentially to the Soo-Machu Picchu alignment at the center point of the first (middle) circle.

---

[43] (41° 54′ 20″ N at 85° 28′ 32″ W)

[44] (42° 25′ 23″ N at 85° 43′ 22″ W)

[45] (42° 54′ 24″ N at 85° 45′ 20″ W)

[46] centered near 42° 56′ 58″ N at 85° 42′ 35″ W

[47] (43° 51′ 04″ N at 85° 02′ 01″ W)

[48] (43° 55′ 23″ N at 85° 09′ 29″ W)

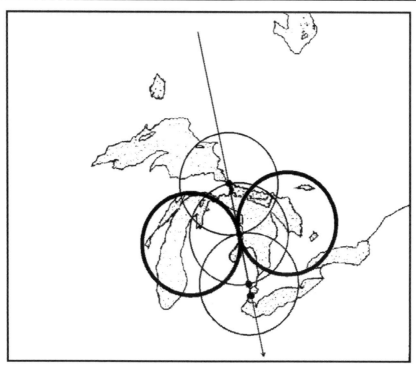

THE FOURTH AND FIFTH CIRCLES

Let us begin by forming the fourth circle on the left of our picture. To achieve the tangency desired, we must set the center point of this circle[49] a few miles south by southwest of the City of Manistee, the seat of Manistee County. The name "Manistee" originates from the Ojibwe name of the principal river of the county, a word that may be derived from *ministigweyaa*, meaning "river with islands at its mouth." In its economic heyday of the late 1800s, Manistee emerged as the home of the booming lumber and shingle manufacturing industries. Today, Manistee maintains popularity through fishing and tourism. Its salt deposits also have made Manistee the home of three salt factories of the Packaging Corporation of America, Morton Salt and Martin Marietta. (Note: Three of the Great Lakes, Lake Michigan, Lake Huron, and Lake Erie, originally were the sites

---

[49] (44° 11' 25" N at 86° 20' 51" W)

of inland seas. After the retreat of glaciers at the end of the last Ice Age, the Great Lakes emerged as freshwater bodies.) Extending the radius eastward, the end point of this line passes within a half mile of a mound located south of the city of Au Gres in Arenac County.[50] From here, we head out and over the Saginaw Bay.

Returning to land, we pass within four miles of multiple mounds[51] that are located in Bay County, north of Bay City. Proceeding inland, we pass through the midst of a region that contains numerous individual mounds as well as mound groupings. These sites are located in and northwest of the city of Owasso in Shiawassee County.[52]

Further west, we pass between three clusters of mounds surrounding Richland, Michigan, in northern Kalamazoo County.[53] A short distance further, we inscribe our line near mounds in northern Kalamazoo County[54] before heading out over Lake Michigan.

Returning to land, we proceed into Wisconsin. There are many significant Pre-Columbian points in this state, among them the well-known Wehmhoff Effigy mound in Racine County.[55] We pass nine miles from this mound. From here, we fly over some beautiful and remote areas of northern Wisconsin and the Upper Peninsula of Michigan, passing nine miles north of the City of Manistique through the town of Hiawatha. For the past three decades, this area has played home to the Hiawatha Traditional Music Festival during the summer.

---

[50] (44° 01′ 54″ N at 83° 41′ 03″ W)
[51] centered at 43° 42′ 27″ N at 83° 18′ 34″ W
[52] centered at 43° 05′ 07″ N at 83° 44′ 16″ W
[53] (42° 24′ 37″ N at 85° 09′ 57″ W)
[54] (42° 21′ 25″ N at 85° 33′ 37″ N) and (42° 20′ 30″ N at 85° 38′ 35″ W)
[55] (42° 4′1 32″ N at 88° 16′ 48″ N)

The historical Hiawatha, a great orator, is believed to have lived five hundred years ago (or perhaps earlier). He was a leader of the Onondaga and Mohawk nations. Native legends tell us that Hiawatha was a follower of the Great Peacemaker, a prophet and spiritual leader who is credited as the founder of the Iroquois confederacy. From its New York homeland, the confederacy aggressively enlarged its territorial control to include much of Ontario, Québec, Pennsylvania, Ohio, and Michigan.

Once again, we cross the lake and pass a couple of miles south of Mackinac City.[56] When Europeans first arrived at the Straits of Mackinac in the 1600s, they found three predominant Algonquian tribes: the Chippewa (Ojibwe), Ottawa (Odawa), and Potawatomi. These tribes frequented the area to fish, hunt, trade, and worship. Mackinac Island, which lies within the straits separating the lower and upper peninsulas of Michigan, appeared to have the shape of a giant turtle, an animal that the Mackinac tribe believed contributed to the beginning of life.

According to legend, Mackinac Island was created by Michabou, the Great Hare. The island served as a gathering place for the local tribes, who made offerings to Gitche Manitou and buried their chiefs in sacred ground. Continuing southward, we complete this circle at the point at which we began.

Finally, we draw the fifth circle on the right side of our map. Let us center this circle at a location off the coast in the Georgian Bay.[57] This location is about twenty-one miles due north of the harbor town of Wiarton in Bruce County, Ontario. Extending the radius eastward, we enter Haliburton County, which is located in the heart of an area containing thousands of small

---

[56] (54° 44′ 27″ N at 84° 45′ 27″ W)
[57] (45° 02′ 35″ N at 81° 06′ 59″ W)

lakes. Today, this region, which is fifty thousand square miles long, is known as a tourist and cottage industry area due to its scenery and the proliferation of resident artists.

Moving clockwise, we pass along the shoreline of Toronto and inland past the city of Hamilton. Going further, we pass through the city of Woodstock, the seat of Oxford County, which is located along the Thames River. However, this prosperous community, with a West End filled with large Victorian homes, often is eclipsed by nearby Stratford, Ontario, the home of the Stratford Shakespeare Festival.

Proceeding westward through the Pinery Provincial Park, we cross the lower end of Lake Huron and enter the Thumb region of Michigan at Port Sanilac. As we traverse the Thumb of Michigan, we pass by numerous sites noted by W.B. Hinsdale in his *Archaeological Atlas of Michigan*. Again passing over the Saginaw Bay, we return to the region at which we began drawing our five circles. We come ashore at Lake Huron Beach and pass through Alabaster Junction. Onward through Rogers City on the shore of upper Lake Huron, we cross back into Ontario and return to the lake region at which we started.

Chapter 11
VESICA PISCIS

Having completed this necessary set of five circles, we next will create a set of Vesica Piscis lines. A Vesica Piscis is the intersection of two circles with the same radius, intersecting in such a way that the center of each circle lies on the circumference of the other. We will use these lines to generate the inner core of our Sacred Geometry. Many mathematicians view the Vesica Piscis through the portal of philosophy by considering it as an intermediate realm that partakes of both changing and unchanging principles, the ephemeral and the eternal. Philosophy tells us that human consciousness plays the role of mediator, balancing the two complementary poles of consciousness.

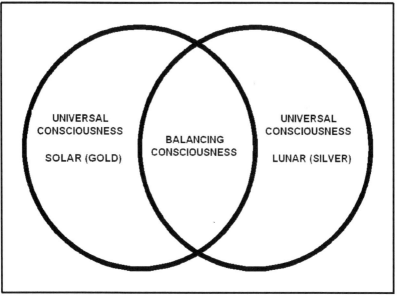

VESICA PISCIS AS BALANCING CONSCIOUSNESS

For a precise rendering of the Great Lakes Biome, we need to complete the next set of steps. First, we insert the Vesica Piscis line at the intersection of the first (middle) and the fifth (right-hand) circles. Next, we add a segment that extends from[58] fourteen miles west by northwest of Elliot Lake in the Algoma District of Ontario southward to a point[59] located a half mile offshore from the Pinery Provincial Park on Lake Huron near Grand Bend, Ontario.

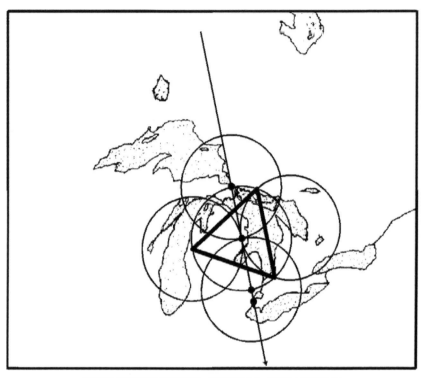

THE FIRST EQUILATERAL TRIANGLE

We will use this length to complete our first equilateral triangle. We do this by drawing two additional lines from the center point of the fourth (left-hand) circle[60] a few miles south by southwest of the City of Manistee. This connects the left end of the upper side of the triangle to the upper end of the Vesica Piscis. Similarly, the lower side of this triangle traverses the end of the lower line to the bottom end of the Vesica Piscis. This

---

[58] (46° 28′ 30″ N at 82° 55′ 44″ W)
[59] (43° 13′ 30″ N at 81° 57′ 54″ W)
[60] at 44° 11′ 25″ N at 86° 20′ 51″ W

produces an equilateral triangle centered at the center point of the first (middle) circle.

Next, we create the opposing triangle. We insert a Vesica Piscis at the intersection of the first (middle) circle and the fourth (left-hand) circle. This segment extends from a barren area[61] of Mackinac County, Michigan, and through the developed end of Beaver Island in Lake Michigan. From 6000 to 2000 BCE, this land was not an island; rather, it was but an appendage of the mainland. Later, the water rose to thirty feet above its present level, submerging all of Beaver Island except the central plateau. From archeological artifacts found on the island, we know that Native Americans passed by it as long ago as 200 BCE. We continue this line southward through Mount Pleasant, home of the Clarke Historical Library (which contains a fine collection of Native American, prehistoric, and archeological materials), to a point[62] north of East Lansing, Michigan, in southeastern Clinton County. As mentioned earlier, this area contains the greatest concentration of mounds in the state — fifty-seven in all. In his book *Primitive Man in Michigan* (unknown, 1925), Dr. W. B. Hinsdale wrote, "There are fully 600 mounds still to be seen in the state and at least 500 more must have been destroyed within the last 150 years." Based upon evidence of uncovered artifacts, some archaeologists believe that the earliest mound-builders entering the Bronze Age had a high level of intelligence and traded with the Aztecs and Mayans.

---

[61] 46° 02′ 15″ N at 85° 37′ 06″ W

[62] 42° 48′ 40″ N at 84° 30′ 56″ W

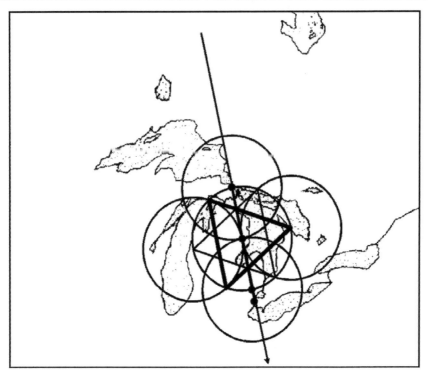

THE SECOND TRIANGLE

We use this segment to complete a second equilateral triangle. The end points of the two additional sides converge at the center point of the fifth (right-side) circle[63] in the Manitoulin District of Georgian Bay.

Finally, we insert the Vesica Pisces in the intersection of the top and fourth (left-hand) circles and continue this line through the intersection of the bottom and fifth (right-hand) circles. This forms a continuous diagonal. Both this line and the next are 374.1 miles in length. We run our first Red Line from a point in a wooded area near the Escanaba River this is approximately eighteen miles north of the City of Escanaba and thirty-eight miles south of the City of Marquette at the edge of the ancient

---

[63] (45° 02′ 31″ N at 81° 06′ 32″ W)

copper region.[64] Progressing southeast, we pass through the Charlevoix/Boyne City resort area and through the center point of the first circle. We continue over Lake Huron to a wooded area that is located about a half mile north of Creditville and seven miles east of Woodstock in Oxford County, Ontario.[65]

---

[64] (45° 02′ 31″ N at 81° 06′ 32″ W)
[65] (43° 09′ 30″ N at 80° 36′ 39″ W)

Chapter 12
SOLOMON'S KEY

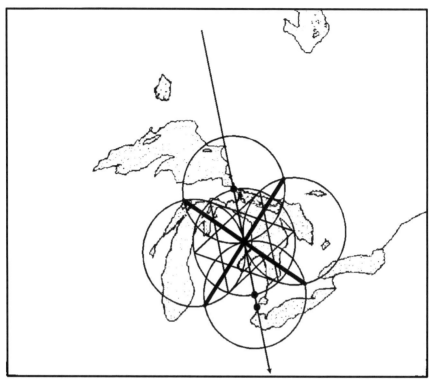

THE EMERGENCE OF SOLOMON'S KEY

We replicate this action by drawing the Vesica Piscis line through the intersection of the top and fifth (right-side) circle. We continue this line through the intersection of the bottom and fourth (left-hand) circle to form another diagonal line. We commence our second line from a point forty miles northwest of the Garson Nickel mines, Lake Wanapitei, and the Sudbury meteorite craters.[66] Progressing southwest, we pass over northern Ontario, Lake Huron, the center of the first circle, and Mount Pleasant. Then we continue past the mound groupings of Grand Rapids, Michigan, until we end this diagonal on some farmland at the outskirts of Kalamazoo. At this end, we find

---

[66] (46° 55' 20" N at 81° 38' 31" W)

ourselves at the northeast corner of West G Ave. and North 7th Street in an area surrounded by mounds and earthworks that was described by Dr. Hinsdale. At this point,[67] we are within seven miles of the Northwood, Oshtemo, Bronson Park, and Cooper mounds. The completion of these two axes creates a generative shape in Sacred Geometry that is known as Solomon's Key. Referred to as both "The Key" and "Solomon's Key," this piece of Sacred Geometry has a long history. As we shall find momentarily, its history extends far back in time to the ancient world.

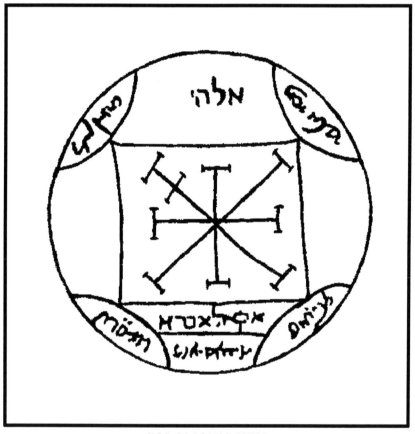

SOLOMON'S KEY

---

[67] (42° 19′ 58″ N at 85° 41′ 42″ W)

Next, we sketch in a line that lies perpendicular to the Soo-Machu Picchu alignment and forms the diameter of the first circle. We use the length of this line to create lines that run tangent to quarter-points along the first circle. This creates the shape of an open-ended square that contains four equal sections.

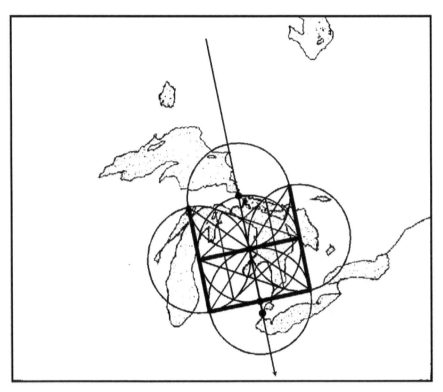

COMPLETING SOLOMON'S KEY

By using Solomon's Key, we can determine a number of quintessential measures, including the relative lengths of *phi*. We start by inscribing a line from the center point at the Soo and continuing it to the lower right-had corner of the square located at the point that the bottom and fifth (right-side) circles intersect.

Chapter 13
GENERATING PHI

Determining the proportion of *phi* is essential for generating the shape of the Great Lakes Biome pattern. In Sacred Geometry, the generation of phi comes from the measurement of the diagonal of a rectangle having sides of the proportion of 2:1.

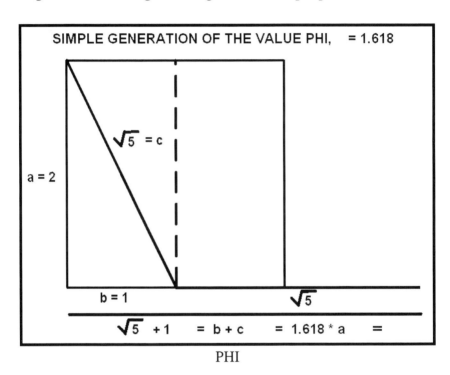

SIMPLE GENERATION OF THE VALUE PHI, ϕ = 1.618

$\sqrt{5}$ = c

a = 2

b = 1

$\sqrt{5}$

$\sqrt{5}$ + 1 = b + c = 1.618 * a = ϕ

PHI

Starting at the Soo, we draw a line to either of the two opposite corners of the square. In this rendition, our line follows a path to the Woodstock area of Ontario. Though this line does not represent the measure of *phi*, we will use it to generate a length of *phi*. For the moment, we use this diagonal as a radius to generate a larger circle that sets inside and tangent to the primary pentagon that will be generated. The five sides of this Great Lakes Biome pentagon will lay tangent to this circle.

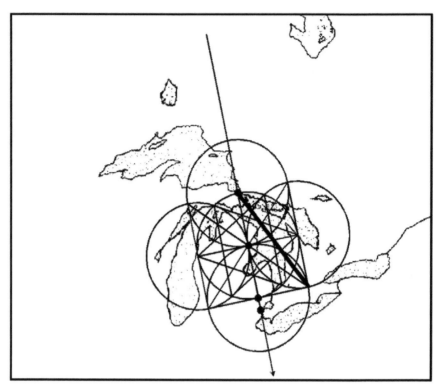

THE DIAGONAL FOR GENERATING *PHI*

This radius measures 295.77 miles in length. We rotate it clockwise to inscribe the interior circle. Starting our circumference at a point due east, we inscribe our circle through southern Ontario, across Lake St. Clair, into the Straits of Detroit (aka the Detroit River). Then, we trace along the length of Belle Isle.

Belle Isle, Detroit's island park, has gone through a series of name changes across the centuries. The island is important for marking the alignment between the two vast copper regions mined in ancient times, the first along the shores of Lake Superior in North America and the second in the Peruvian Andes. One of the markers that existed along this line may have been in Detroit, an area that constitutes one of the three primary crossing points in the Great Lakes region. Detroit is important for another reason as well: it is the only point other than the Soo that falls upon the Soo-Machu Picchu alignment. The marker or markers may have been ancient sacred mounds or stones that once existed.

In the tale of "The Cross and the Manitou" that she retold in *Legends of Le Detroit* (unknown, 1884), Marie Caroline Watson Hamlin relates one of the historically supportable legends about the destruction of a totem dedicated to the god Manitou by early explorers, the missionaries Francois Doilier de Casson and Abbe Brehant de Galinee. (Note: another totem to Manitou also existed as a sacred tree in the vicinity of the Soo.)

Hamlin recounted, "It was in the early spring of 1670 that their canoes landed at Detroit. [De Casson and de Galinee] came upon an open clearing in the center of which arose a grassy mound crowned by a rude stone idol. It was a crude production of nature, created by her in a tit of abstraction and which the Indians had attempted to convert into the semblance of a deity by touches of vermillion. Offerings of tobacco, skins of animals, and articles of food were scattered in reckless profusion at its feet. This, then, was the great Manitou, of whom their guides had spoken, who held in his hand the winds.... The missionaries, indignant at this exhibition of idolatry, broke the statue in a thousand pieces, and in its place erected a cross, at whose foot they affixed the coat of arms of France.... Taking the largest fragment of the broken idol, the missionaries lashed two canoes together and towed it to the deepest part of the river so that it should be heard of no more. But the tradition says that after the fathers were far away, a band of Indians coming to offer their homage to the deity found only its mutilated remains. Each took a fragment which he placed in his canoe as a fetish, and it guided them to where the Spirit of the Manitou had taken refuge under the deep, sombre, shadow of Belle Isle. He bade them bring every fragment of his broken image and to strew them on the banks of his abode. They obeyed his order, and behold! each stone was converted into a rattlesnake, which should be as a sentinel to guard the sacredness of his domain from the profaning foot of the white man." If we recall, Professor Hinsdale noted the location of a mound that stood about .75 miles northeast of our marking point at Saints Peter and Paul Jesuit Church along Jefferson Avenue. However, as Hinsdale made his observations at a time when the land in the city center already had been developed, there may have been other vanished mounds and markers that he could not document.

Going past the site of the former Great Mound of the Rouge as well as some lesser mounds of the twenty-six that once stood in Detroit and Wayne County, we pass within a mile of three archeological sites on the northeast side of Ann Arbor. Continuing through the towns of Grass Lake and Jackson, we pass a square earthworks and a mound just south of the city of Marshall. We then move onward through an area of seven mounds and earthworks in and southwest of Battle Creek, a city made famous by Dr. John Harvey Kellogg through his cereal and sanitarium.[68]

---

[68] The group of mounds and earthworks are centered around 42° 15′ 05″ N at 85° 19′ 42″ W.

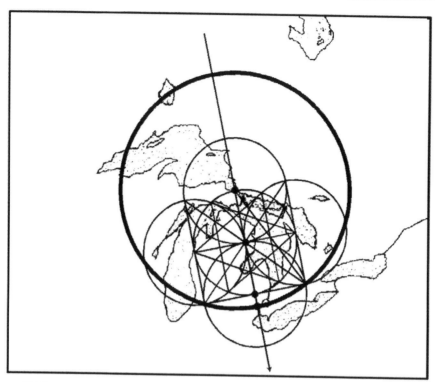

INSCRIBING THE INTERIOR CIRCLE OF THE PENTAGON

After passing through a "constellation" of mounds that are centered at the north end of Kalamazoo,[69] we continue onward toward Lake Michigan. In the process, we travel 3.5 miles south by southwest of a group of four mounds north of Gobles and then two miles north of a pair of mound located a few miles east of the resort area of South Haven.

On the west side of Lake Michigan, we cross the Rennes-le-Chateau parallel in the Wisconsin town of West Allis which is south of Milwaukee. Proceeding northward, we pass through a region that contains several mounds: the Lizard, the Sheboygan, the High Cliff, the Koshkong, the Kingley Bend, and the Vilas Circle Effigy, among others.[70]

---

[69] in the vicinity of 42° 19′ 11″ N at 85° 36′ 47″ W
[70] centered around 43° 39′ 29″ N at 88° 51′ 11″ W

We know more about the mounds of Wisconsin than those in Michigan, thanks to the expedition of William H. Keating that was conducted in 1823. At the time, Keating was a professor of mineralogy and chemistry at the University of Pennsylvania. In 1823, he made an expedition to the Minnesota River, Red River, Lake Winnepeg, Lake of the Woods, and Lake Superior, discovering mounds there before they were razed for agriculture. Historians credit Keating with having produced the earliest written record of the Wisconsin mounds.

As we circle around the corner of the Biome pentagon at the city of Duluth, we pass over Madeline, Stockton, and the Outer Islands that are located in the Copper Region developed by an ancient mining culture in Ontario, north of Lake Superior.

At one time, the body of water that we refer to currently as Lake Superior once was more expansive. Passing through the Grand Marais in Cook County, Minnesota, we enter the region that the Ojibwe referred to as *Kitchi Bitobig*—the double body of water. From here, we pass into Canada. Near the point that will emerge as the northwest tangent point of this circle due north of Isle Royale,[71] we find Lake Nipigon, sometimes called the sixth of the Great Lakes. In a past millennium, the current Lake Nipigon was joined with Lake Superior.

Further east, we find the next point of tangency on the northeast side of the pentagon in the middle of the Moose River watershed that flows into the southern tip of Hudson Bay.[72] Beyond this point, in what will emerge as the northeast corner of our pentagon, we find the CEGEP Institute (*Collège d'enseignement général et professionnel*, meaning "College of General and Vocational Education") that specializes in mining and forestry. As noted earlier, this region has contained

---

[71] at 49° 11′ 21″ N at 89° 20′ 31″ W
[72] (50° 27′ 07″ N at 81° 49′ 14″ W)

substantial deposits of gold and silver. As we head in a southerly direction back to our starting point, we pass within 3.5 miles northwest of the Ghost Island Mounds, which are located in the lake region of middle Ontario.

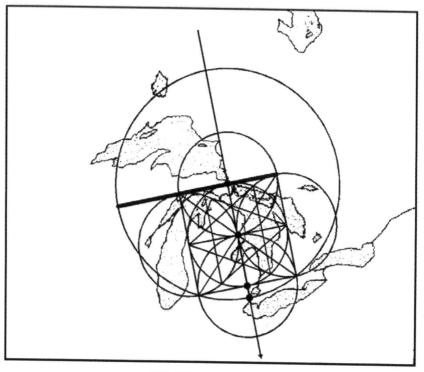

GENERATING *PHI*

We rotate the radius of the circle until it lines up with the upper left-hand corner of the inscribed square. Next, we add a short segment to the top upper-right side of the square. For the purpose of constructing the outer pentagon that touches Duluth, Minnesota, the base of Lake Michigan, and the Niagara River, the length of these two combined pieces equals the determination that we will refer to as *"phi."* However, this is not the same as the standard of ϕ(1.618...). Our relative value *phi* will serve to create other values that we need by using the multiplier divided by the divisor of ϕ.

Now we can begin to construct our figure. By adding the radius of the top circle centered at the Soo — 132.28 miles — to the radius of the large circle that we just inscribed — 295.77 miles, we calculate our value of *phi* as equal to 428.05 miles. We will use this length for constructing each side of the outer Biome pentagon.[73]

---

[73] Note: The default setting on the Google Earth ruler for miles at two decimal places.

Chapter 14
CREATING THE PENTAGON
(ONE OF MANY WAYS TO SKIN A CAT)

We have a few different ways to proceed. Since our goal is to generate a precise rendering of the pentagon and pentangle, we need to establish points of tangency along the circle that we just completed that exist at the mid-point of each side of the pentagon. In addition, we need to establish the corner points of the pentagon accurately. Thus far, we have set the mid-point of the base of the pentagon at Detroit. The major challenge that we face is to compensate for the curvature of the earth over the large surface area of the Great Lakes Region. However, if we establish equally spaced lines that radiate from the Soo, this will help us to maintain the necessary precision. In effect, we will generate a series of concentric pentagons and pentangles of increasing size in order to reach this goal.

First, we copy the line of length *phi* and center it as the Vesica Piscis of the top and first (middle) Circles.

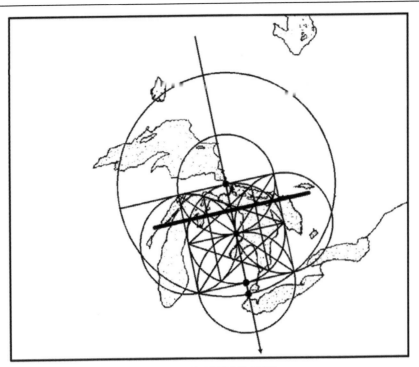

DUPLICATING *PHI*

This line serves as our working length *phi*. Each side of the inscribed square equals unity. We begin by connecting a series of broken lines of a length equal to unity to each end of this new *phi* line while connecting the opposite ends of the two broken lines to a point along the Soo-Machu Picchu alignment just north of our Orion point. One way to complete the pentagon is to extend guidelines of length ϕ(1.618...) from the intersection of the first two broken lines through the upper corners of the inner triangles at the point where the left-hand and right-hand circles intersect the first circle. By extending these guidelines, their end points will lie at the upper two corners of the broken-line pentagon.

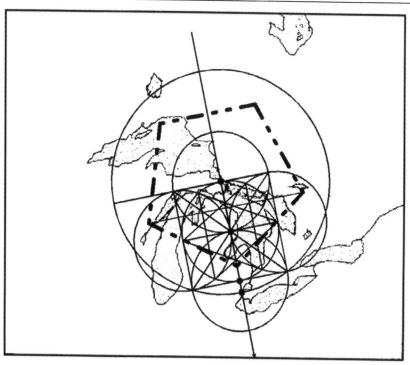

INNER PENTAGON

Our next step is to complete a pentangle within the broken-line pentagon that we just drew. By drawing a series of five lines that radiate from the center point at the Soo through each of the five points of this pentangle (i.e., the corners of our pentagon), we will mark the exact points of tangency on the circle for our large pentagon. As we noted in Chapter Thirteen, the length of our *phi* segment equals 428.05 miles. Dividing this length by ϕ (1.618...), produces the length of the side of the inner broken-line pentagon, 264.55 miles. Reversing the calculation produces 428.05 miles, the length of the side of the inner inverse pentangle.

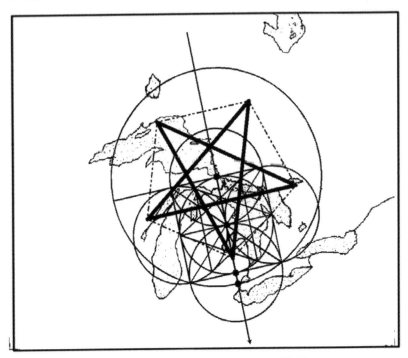

INNER INVERSE PENTANGLE

Building the diagram in this manner may seem a bit complex. However, this method (with the use of Google Earth or a standard globe) helps to ensure that we translate the measurements accurately from a spherical Earth to our flat, two-dimensional renderings. Thus far, we have created numerous guide points in order to extend the following five equidistant radii. Each of these radii measures 295.77 miles. In the following diagram, we find the five radii drawn through the outer points of the inner inverse pentangle and connect them to the circle. This step establishes the precise locations of the points at which the principal Great Lakes Biome Pentagon lays tangent to the circle.

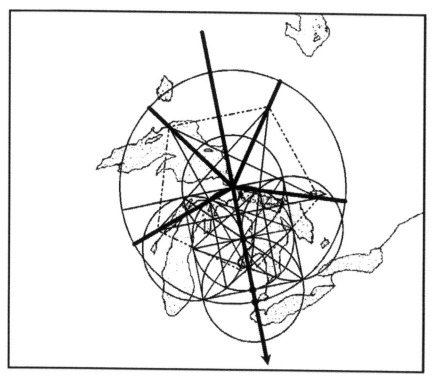

CONNECTING THE SPOKES TO THE WHEEL

In our next step, we inscribe an inverted pentangle within the circle. The points of this new pentangle fall on the tangency points described at the ends of the five radii just drawn. This pentangle serves as a guide for inscribing other pentangles and pentagons and for finding additional locations and alignments within the Biome and beyond. We will find these other locations throughout Europe, Africa, and Asia as well as in North and South America. There *is* method to our madness! The length of the sides of this new pentangle equals 132.28 miles, the length of the radius of any of the original five circles times ϕ^3 (4.249). This equals the length of 562.09 miles.

To some observers, it may seem a bit obsessive to determine our distances to the accuracy of .01 miles (about fifty-three feet). However, extending one of these radii from the Soo to Machu

Picchu magnifies any error significantly. Furthermore, when we extend these patterns around the world, we want to remain as precise as possible in our measurements—spot on, as the British say--to support any assertion that our alignments are more than just casually found phenomena. It is important to note that we are not looking for random alignments. We are looking for multiple points that are related significantly to one another by a *repeated fixed measure.*

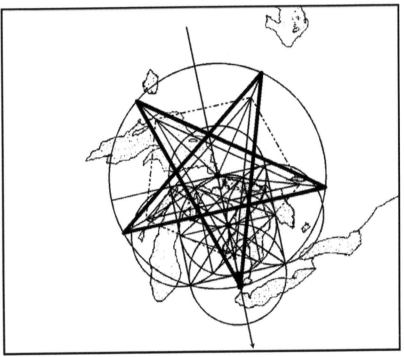

THE OUTER INVERSE PENTANGLE

Connecting the five points of this new pentangle to another with a second set of broken lines produces a second pentagon. This pentagon will serve as a guide for further rendering as well as the roadbed for at least one noticeable pathway. The side of this pentagon has a length that is equal to the side of the pentangle, with segments of 562.09 miles in length divided by ϕ(1.618…). This produces a length of 346.30 miles.

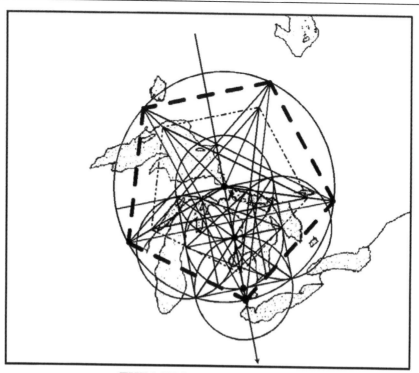

THE MIDDLE PENTAGON

Using the line segment of our calculated length *phi*, we now can complete the major pentagon of the Great Lakes Biome. The length of each side of this new pentagon is the same as each of the five lines of the innermost pentangle. Furthermore, the sides of this new pentagon lay parallel to their corresponding lines of the two innermost pentangles. We set each line of the new pentagon at their respective tangent points along the outer circle (i.e., the points at which the outermost pentangle touch the circle). Drawing guidelines through the inner corners of the two inverse pentangles from the center point at the Soo aids us to locate the five corners of the outer pentagon visually. Extended northward from the Soo, the original Soo-Machu Picchu alignment provides a guideline for setting the two northern sides of the major pentagon in a way that ensures that the point of tangency on the large circle falls at the precise mid-point of these lines, forming the sides of the major pentagon.

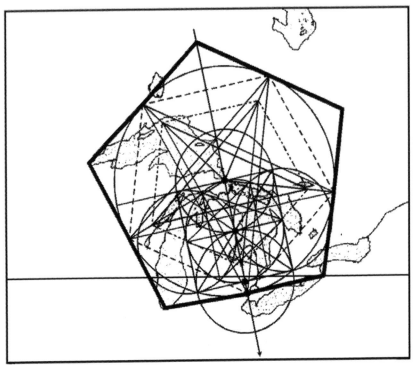

THE OUTER PENTAGON

With the addition of an upright pentangle with points touching the five corners of the major pentagon, we complete our basic diagram of the Great Lakes Biome. This derivation includes a pentagon and pentangle that virtually are identical to those originally sketched by Peter Champoux in 2002. The length of each of the line segments of the upright pentangle equals 428.05 miles times 1.618. The result equals 692.58 miles. In conclusion, our completed derivation of the Great Lakes Biome diagram includes all of the primary points, circles, and segments of the underlying Sacred Geometry.

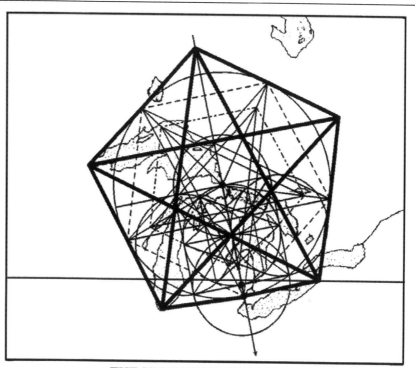

THE UPRIGHT PENTANGLE

Chapter 15
REFLECTIONS IN A GOLDEN EYE

Numerous researchers across many disciplines have asserted that ancient cultures drew lines upon the earth and placed structures at critical points along these lines. These alignments often reflect groupings of stars and planets that appear in the night sky. Though drawing constellations remains culturally subjective, philosophers, scientists, and others have given a great deal of attention to the pattern that western culture refers to as the constellation of Orion, and especially to the three bright stars referred to as Orion's Belt. *A priori,* while laboring within the context of Sacred Geometry, I knew that the stylized shape of this constellation can be derived from a set of sacred geometric forms. Therefore, let us return to the matter of Orion introduced in Chapter Four.

Many stars exist in the sky. Which ones meet the criteria for inclusion in what we may describe as Culturally Iconic Constellations? Perhaps humans have chosen from among those stars, planets, and satellites that are the easiest to locate with the naked eye and that fit stylistically into the patterns of Sacred Geometry. As a result, these astral objects have served the needs of measurement for navigation, hunting, agriculture, ceremony, architecture and other activities of life for a very long time.

If we take a star map of the area of the sky that includes the Constellation Orion, we can find a few curiosities. When humans have constructed series of pyramids or churches that have patterns that reflects constellations, these patterns are not taken from the perspective of what we see when we look at the sky directly. Rather, these patterns are reflectios of the sky that one might see in a still pond of water. In the construction trade, such a reverse drawing is used for setting ceiling tiles—a reflected ceiling plan.

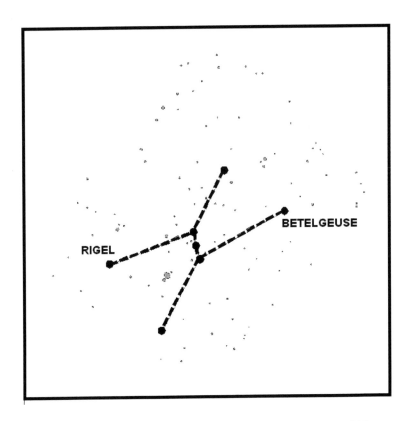

REFLECTION OF THE ORION CONSTELLATION

In order to obtain this perspective of Orion, let us take a transparent star map and flip it horizontally. Next, we will rotate the reflected sky map to the point that Orion's Belt sets upon the Soo-Machu-Picchu alignment along our original three center points at the Soo, mid-Michigan, and Lake Orion. Finally, by using our derived Sacred Geometry of the Great Lakes Biome, we will replicate the lines extending from Orion's Belt to four stars--Betelgeuse, Rigel, and two others of prominence.

Though our rendering is stylized, the geometry will serve another purpose later in our exploration. Our three original center points form Orion's Belt. Next, we inscribe the path to the star known as Rigel by drawing a line from the Soo through a point on the southwest side of the pentagon, which is located at three-eighths of *phi* (the length of a side of the major pentagon) from the Lake Superior-Duluth corner.

Second, we will inscribe the path to the reflection of the star known as Betelgeuse by drawing a line from the center point at Orion, Michigan eastward through a point located at one-fourth of *phi* from the southeast corner of the pentagon, which is located at the headwater of the Niagara River. The next path in our constellation diagram starts at the Soo and travels north by northeast through the midpoint of the northeast side of the pentangle. Finally, our last path starts at the Orion, Michigan, point and extends through the base of the pentagon at a distance of one-sixteenth of *phi* west of Detroit.

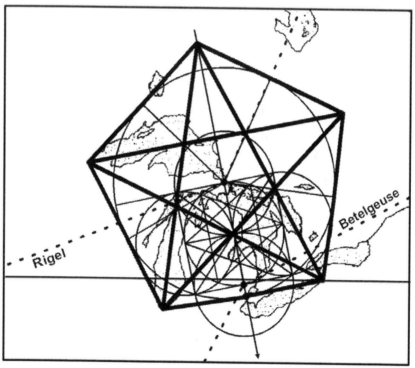

REFLECTION OF ORION SUPERIMPOSED ON THE BIOME

The completion of this task gives us the reflected Orion pattern, which is superimposed on our drawing of the Great Lakes Biome. This may be more than a pretty picture, since there are global connections to these Orion lines as well as to a number of the other lines in the Biome drawing. For the moment, let us note that the Betelgeuse line passes within fourteen miles of the Ghost Island Mounds in Ontario along the edge of the circle tangent to the major pentagon.

Before proceeding further, we "zoom out" to view the entire Great Lakes region, which also includes southern Ohio. Though ancient mounds and earthworks have been discovered and explored throughout the United States, especially in mid-America from the northern states to the Gulf of Mexico, we find that the two largest known concentrations exist in southern Michigan and southern Ohio. Per calculations based on Professor Hinsdale's observations, these two regions contain an average of one mound per every fifty square miles. However, Hinsdale found most of the mounds in clusters.

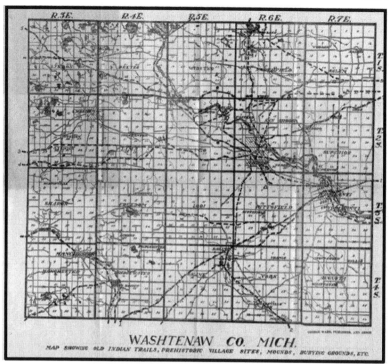

WASHTENAW CO. MICH.

MAP SHOWING OLD INDIAN TRAILS, PREHISTORIC VILLAGE SITES, MOUNDS, BURYING GROUNDS, ETC.

SHEET FROM HINSDALE'S ARCHAEOLOGICAL ATLAS OF 1931

The icons displayed on the following map are based upon the work of Dr. Wilbert B. Hinsdale of the University of Michigan. Hinsdale made these measurements and produced his maps during the first quarter of the twentieth century. The plotting of the Hinsdale sites into layers in Google Earth is an ongoing project that is performed by historian James Porter and other members of the Google Earth Users Community. The overlays are available for download at google.com. In addition, we credit anthropologist/archaeologist   James   Q.   Jacobs (http://www.jqjacobs.net) for his extensive efforts in this field.

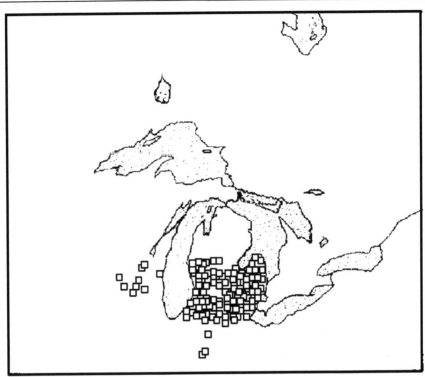

CONCENTRATION OF MOUNDS IN SOUTHERN MICHIGAN

Chapter 16
ADDING SOME MORE DETAILS

Now we can add a few more features to our regional diagram that overlays Sacred Geometry on the Great Lakes Biome. Three primary routes of travel have existed in their current locations at least since the time of the Hopewell civilization. These paths radiate outward from what is now downtown (city center) Detroit. Enough historical information exists in the early records that were maintained by French missionaries and military to refute the notion that the radial plan of Detroit is based merely on the design of Paris, Washington, D.C., or other cities. The evidence suggests that these major radial paths have been well-beaten for more than a millennium.

The three major routes meander slightly as they cross the State of Michigan. Nevertheless, as can be demonstrated with the use of the linear regression technique borrowed from the field of Statistics, these paths tightly follow trajectories that are evident in the Biome diagram.

The baseline of the major pentagon extends through its midpoint in Detroit and continues to the base of Lake Michigan near Chicago. Now known as Michigan Avenue and M-12, this path was called the Chicago Road a century ago. However, in earlier centuries explorers referred to it as the Sauk Trail. It led from encampments of Pottawatomie, Ojibwa, Huron, and other earlier inhabitants of Southeast Michigan to major encampments of the Sauk and Fox tribes at the base of Lake Michigan. However, the initial settlement of this area developed many millennia earlier as the glaciers receded from the Great Lakes.[74]

---

[74] Oldlighthousemuseum.org, citation contributed by Jason T. Schlenkert

The second path also follows a route from Detroit through the lower part of the state. This path passes through the Grand River Valley in Lansing and onward through Grand Rapids to Lake Michigan. The remnants of the largest concentration of mounds in Michigan lie along this path. They are within Clinton County and in and around Grand Rapids, where there is another series of mounds. The trajectory line that follows this path lies along the southwest side of the larger of the two broken-line pentagons in our original drawing. Continuing along this trajectory takes us within twenty-two miles of Chippewa Falls, a site noted by Peter Champoux in his diagram as an ancient sacred meeting ground. From this point, the path leads onward to the middle of the Minneapolis metropolitan area.

A third path follows Woodward Avenue (Detroit's main street) outward from the city center. This heads north by northwest through Pontiac, Michigan. The ancient path now known as Woodward Avenue was christened as such the morning after the Great Fire of 1805, a fire that destroyed the entire city. Territorial Governor Hull and Judge Augustus Woodward, the legal presence in old Detroit, appeared that morning with a completed plan for the new city (see the diagram in Chapter Eight). Their radial street plan, which resembled other radial city plans, would be overlaid upon the existing major trade routes and well-beaten paths of antiquity. Judge Woodward declared that this widened main street (made possible by the fire) should be renamed Woodward Avenue because it proceeded "northward toward the woods." Many observers believe in the possibility that Woodward really named it for himself. One can follow the extension of this path through what once had been the encampment of Chief Pontiac's Ottawa tribe north of Detroit and onward to the Grand Traverse region. This path continues past Copper Harbor and Manitou Island at the tip of the Keweenaw Peninsula. We can trace this path by inscribing a line from the midpoint of the baseline of the major pentagon[75] to the midpoint of its northwest side,[76] a line that runs parallel to the southwest side of the pentagon.

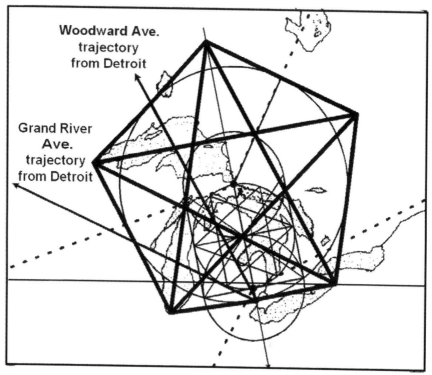

WOODWARD AND GRAND RIVER AVENUE TRAJECTORIES

This present exploration remains a work in progress, since more and more curious alignments and sites are being discovered. Therefore, let us turn our attention outward and look for significant sites beyond the Great Lakes Biome. To begin, let us look at a larger overview of the paths that emanate from the Soo and extend through the corners, mid-points, and quarter-points of the major pentagon.

---

[75] (42° 19' 55" N at 83° 02' 17" W)
[76] (49° 11' 21" N at 89° 20' 31" W)

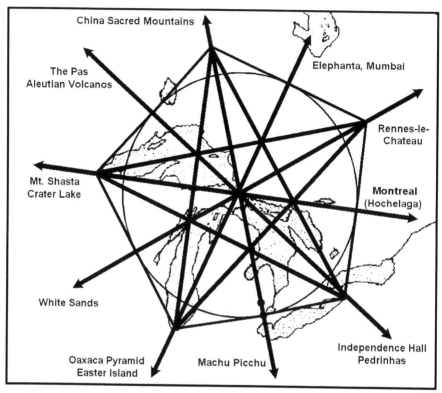

TEN RADII

Line One:

To begin our journey, let us proceed clockwise from the first arrow to the left of the Soo-Machu Picchu alignment. This first line runs south by southwest. It passes the Towosaghy Pyramid at Wolf Island[77] and Lilbourn Mound, an ancient palisade town with a large central mound, smaller mounds, and a plaza that carbon dates from 1,260 CE.[78] In Missouri, we find Chucalissa Village, an ancient settlement built between 1,000 and 1,500

---

[77] (36° 41' 39" N at 89° 14' 06" W)
[78] (36° 34' 19" N at 89° 35' 18" W)

CE.[79] We then encounter the Poverty Point Earthworks, a Pre-Columbian archeological site in northeastern Louisiana[80] that dates back to 1650 – 700 BCE. Crossing the Gulf of Mexico, we return to land and pass through the Oaxaca region of Mexico, which is 2,152 miles from the Soo. We find ourselves within 2.5 miles of the Oaxaca Pyramid and the ruins atop Mount Alban[81] as well as the Mayan ruins at Mitla.[82] The earliest construction at this site dates to 200 CE. By 500 BCE, Mitla was occupied.

MOUNT ALBAN IN OAXACA, MEXICO

Continuing along this line to a coordinate that is 5,300 miles from the Soo, we land on Easter Island, aka Rapa Nui.[83] Here we can find the 887 monumental statues called *moai* that were created by the Rapanui people sometime after 400 CE.

---

[79] (35° 03' 30" N at 90° 07' 42"W)

[80] (32° 38' 09" N at 91° 24' 14" W)

[81] (17° 02' 38" N at 96° 46' 06" W)

[82] (16° 55' 01" N at 96° 24' 01" W)

[83] (27° 07' 16"S at 109° 21' 59" W)

THE MOAI OF EASTER ISLAND

Line Two:

Located 1,490 miles from the Soo along our second line, we enter the region of White Sands in south-central New Mexico. Here we find the largest fields of gypsum sand in the world:[84] brilliant white dunes cover an area of nearly 230 square miles. The dunes have been a fabled site for vision quests by Native Americans from throughout the southwest and northern Mexico. Though National Park and government officials resolutely deny the existence of UFOs, visitors claim to have sighted hundreds of them at White Sands over the past thirty years.

---

[84] (32° 53′ 30″ N at 106° 18′ 12″ W)

WHITE SANDS, NEW MEXICO

Line Three:

Our third line takes us to the mid-point between Mount Shasta and Crater Lake, 1,880 miles from the Soo. At Mount Shasta,[85] the oldest known human habitation dates to 5000 BCE. By 3000 BCE, substantial settlements had developed in the surrounding area. Since ancient times, Native Americans have considered Shasta a sacred site. In modern times, Guy Ballard's I Am Activity (1930s) and Elizabeth Clare Prophet's Church Universal and Triumphant (1950s) have emerged as the best-known of the numerous groups participating in Shasta's spiritual heritage. Some cults maintain that races of sentient or spiritual beings such as Lemurians live in or on Shasta or visit it regularly.

---

[85] (41° 24′ 26″N at 122° 11′ 37″ W)

MOUNT SHASTA

CRATER LAKE

Crater Lake[86] sit 105 miles North of Mount Shasta. Around 5700 BCE, a massive volcanic eruption led to the subsidence of Mount Mazama and the emergence of the lake. Later, lava eruptions created a central platform known as Wizard Island,

---

[86] (42° 56′ 23″N at 122° 06′ 03″ W)

along with other features. The Klamath Tribe, a group that may have witnessed the formation of Crater Lake, continues to regard the lake as a sacred site and uses it for vision quests. The tribe considers those who return from their quests successfully as having great spiritual powers.

Line Four:

As we extend a fourth line from the Soo, we move through "The Pas" (perhaps from pasquia—a Cree word meaning "wooded narrows") in Manitoba.[87] Some researchers have asserted that the Cree, who migrated from the southeastern prairies over 9,000 years ago, were the original inhabitants of the area.

Further along our fourth line, we pass over the Mendenhall Glacier,[88] which was called Aak'wtaaksit ("the Glacier behind the Little Lake") by the Tlingit people. In 1899, it was renamed in honor of the autodidact U.S. physicist and meteorologist Thomas Corwin Mendenhall.

---

[87] (53° 50′ 27″N at 101° 15′ 56″ W)
[88] (58° 26′ 11″N at 133° 44′ 31″ W)

MENDENHALL GLACIER

Heading beyond the mainland, we pass along a chain of active volcanoes. The first volcano that we encounter is Mount Makushin, a strato-volcano that is located on Unalaska Island in the Aleutian Islands. The name Makushin probably is derived from the Russian word *makushka*, which means "the crown (of the head)" or "top."

Secondly, we pass over another strato-volcano, Mount Akutan. It contains a two kilometer-wide caldera with two post-caldera cones, Lava Point and Lava Peak. This second one dates from the Pleistocene Age.

The third volcano of the chain is Mount Okmok, the highest point on the rim of Okmok Caldera on the northeastern part of Umnak Island. Finally, we arrive at Mount Cleveland, a point that is 3,628 miles from the Soo. This symmetrical volcano is one of the most active of those in the Aleutians. It has been the site of numerous eruptions in the last two centuries, the most recent of which occurred in 2005.

Line Five:

Our fifth line takes us over the top of the world and into the midst of China's sacred mountains, which are located approximately 7,000 miles from the Soo. This region of China includes the five Taoist Mountains, the four Buddhist Mountains, and the large grouping of Chinese pyramids. We will explore this area in more detail within Chapter Twenty-Three.

Line Six:

Our sixth line takes us 7,700 miles from the Soo to the heart of the ancient city of Mumbai (formerly Bombay), the capital of the Indian state of Maharashtra. The city proper, the largest in India, is the second most populous city in the world with approximately fourteen million inhabitants. Mumbai is built on what was once an archipelago of seven islands. In 1939, an unnamed British archaeologist suggested that these islands were inhabited since the Stone Age. He stated that their earliest known inhabitants were the Kolis, a fishing community. In the third century BCE, the seven islands formed part of the Maurya Empire.

MUMBAI, INDIA

Line Seven:

Our seventh radius takes us 4,042 miles from the Soo to the village of Rennes-le-Chateau in the Languedoc region of southern France. In the books *The Holy Place: Saunière and the Decoding of the Mystery of Rennes-le-Château* (1991, 2004) by Henry Lincoln and *Genisis: The First Book of Revelations* (1986) by David Wood with Henry Lincoln, the authors thoroughly measured and explored the Sacred Geometry of apparent alignments in this region. The south of France was the home of the Cathars and then the Knights Templar through the 13th century. Many assert it also was home to Mary Magdalene after fleeing the Holy Land in 33 CE. As we will see later in our journey, Tour Magdala (Magdalene Tower) comes into play with a number of key alignments.

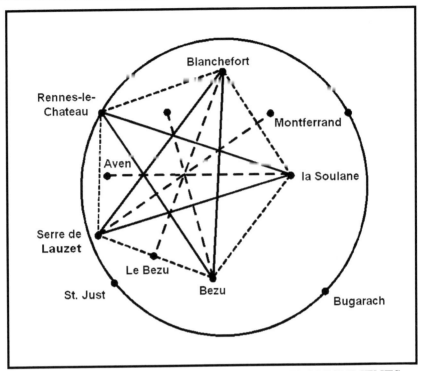

ONE SET OF THE RENNES-LE-CHATEAU ALIGNMENTS

Line Eight:

Drawing our eighth line from the Soo leads us to the south side of Montreal, Canada, at Mount Royal. As noted in the Iintroduction, this site has a history as the Pre-Columbian city of Hochelaga.[89] Archaeological evidence points to the occupation of the island of Montreal by various nomadic native peoples for at least 2,000 years (circa 500 BCE) before the arrival of Europeans in the sixteenth-century. The St. Lawrence Iroquoians established the fortified village of Hochelaga at the foot of Mount Royal. A French expedition led by Jacques Cartier made the first European contact with the Iroquois in 1535.

---

[89] (45° 30′ 00″ N at 73° 35′ 00″ W)

HOCHELAGA

Line Nine:

Our ninth line extending from the Soo carries us past the Ghost Island Burial Mounds in southern Ontario[90] and onward through downtown Philadelphia, the City of Brotherly Love and the home of polymath Benjamin Franklin and other members of the Enlightenment Movement in colonial America. Our path takes us in front of Independence Hall, the U.S. national landmark on Chestnut Street between 5th and 6th Streets.[91] Known primarily as the location where the Declaration of Independence was debated and adopted, it became the principal meeting place of the Second Continental Congress from 1775 to 1783.

---

[90] (44° 36' 01" N at 78° 48' 51" W)
[91] (39° 56' 56" N at 75° 09' 00" W)

INDEPENDENCE HALL, PHILADELPHIA

Along the same line, at a point located 4,904 miles from the Soo, stands a curious stone marker southeast of Pedrinhas, Brazil. Thus far, this marker remains a mystery. Did this formation structure occur naturally? A survey of the area does not indicate a rocky terrain--quite the opposite, in fact. The area contains relatively flat grasslands southeast of a small community. It resembles similar natural monuments left by retreating glaciers much further to the north. Is this edifice an occurrence of nature or did humans construct it?

Line Ten:

Line ten is the alignment of the Soo to Machu Picchu. As a key element of this exploration, we will return to it at a later point.

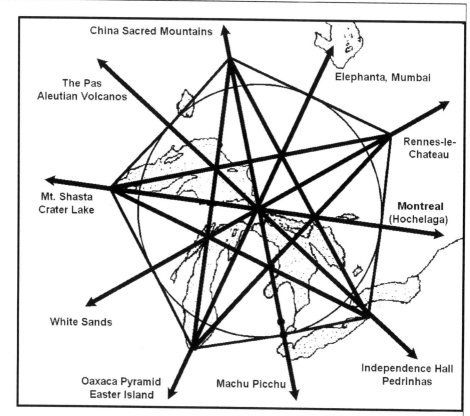

China Sacred Mountains

Elephanta, Mumbai

The Pas
Aleutian Volcanos

Rennes-le-
Chateau

Mt. Shasta
Crater Lake

Montreal
(Hochelaga)

White Sands

Independence Hall
Pedrinhas

Oaxaca Pyramid
Easter Island

Machu Picchu

IN SUMMARY

Chapter 18
THE FRENCH CONNECTIONS

Next, we will inscribe a series of lines that connect the Great Lakes Biome to the European Alaise system of alignments. By extending the four European meridians (discussed earlier) to the north rotational pole and then bringing them down to the Great Lakes at exactly ninety degrees to the original meridians in Europe, we produce the four longitudinal lines connected to the Stonehenge, Greenwich, Paris, and Alaise meridians. The Alaise (Merovingian) line lies slightly east of the Michigan-Ohio meridian and crosses the Soo-Machu Picchu alignment at the mid-point between the Soo and the center point of the first (middle) circle of our Sacred Geometry sketch of the Great Lakes. The Paris line lies on the west side of the Biome, passing along Copper Harbor and Manitou Island. The Greenwich line lies further west and crosses the major pentagon for a second time at the intersection of the Rigel star line. Finally, the Stonehenge line lies furthest to the west and runs tangent to the western corner of the major pentagon.

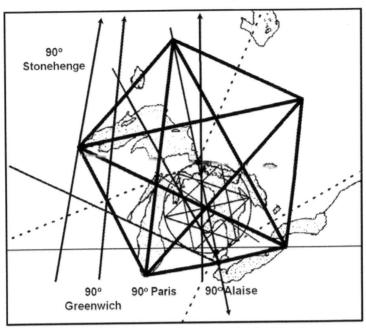

90°
Stonehenge

90°
Greenwich

90° Paris

90° Alaise

AT NINETY DEGREES LONGITUDE
OF EUROPEAN MERIDIANS

Before exploring beyond the Great Lakes region, let us look at the lines that connect the Biome to the geometry surrounding Rennes-le-Chateau, which lies in the ancient Cathar region of France. If we extend a straight path from the Soo that passes through the northeast corner of the pentagon, we find that it arcs over the Earth to the Tour Magdala in the village of Rennes-le-Chateau some 4,042 furlong miles away. Alternately, following the path along the 42° 55′ 38″ N parallel from the Niagara River corner of the Biome to Rennes-le-Chateau takes us a distance of approximately 4,100 miles. For reference, the distance from the Soo to Machu-Picchu is 4,167 miles.

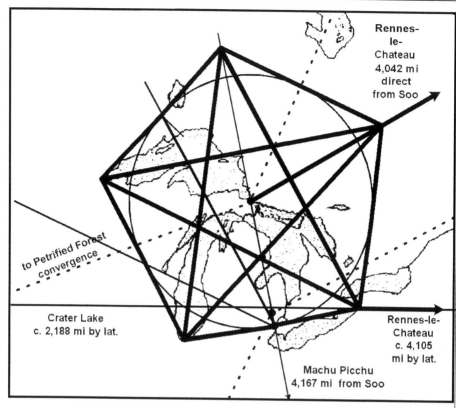

Rennes-
le-
Chateau
4,042 mi
direct
from Soo

to Petrified Forest
convergence

Crater Lake
c. 2,188 mi by lat.

Rennes-le-
Chateau
c. 4,105
mi by lat.

Machu Picchu
4,167 mi from Soo

CONNECTIONS TO RENNES-LE-CHATEAU

Next, let us draw a straight line that arcs over the Earth from a more remote location. Approximately 100 miles east of the Sedona vortices, we find the Petrified Forest and adjacent sites in the Painted Desert of Arizona. Let us mark a point[92] in the strip between the Petrified Forest and an area to the north in Navajo County that looks like a battlefield, possibly pock-marked by a meteor shower. We want to inscribe a line that starts from this point along the Rigel star line extending from the Soo and continues all the way to the site of the ancient holy city of Faras, near the Abu Simbel temple along the Nile.

---

[92] at 35° 11' 31" N at 109° 59' 58" W

135

Chapter 19
DRAWING THE ARC

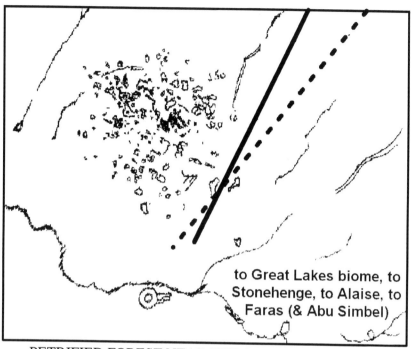

to Great Lakes biome, to Stonehenge, to Alaise, to Faras (& Abu Simbel)

PETRIFIED FOREST NEAR THE SEDONA VORTICES

Starting at the site near the Petrified Forest,[93] we follow the line towards the Great Lakes Biome. As we progress, we notice that our path touches the northern corner of the Great Lakes Biome pentagon, which is north of Lake Superior. Continuing, we arc over the globe past Hudson Bay, along the southern tip of Greenland,[94] through County Wicklow, Ireland, and onward to England.

---

[93] (39° 19′ 36″ N at 109° 52′ 08″ W)

[94] (59° 26′ 26″ N at 43° 56′ 17″ W)

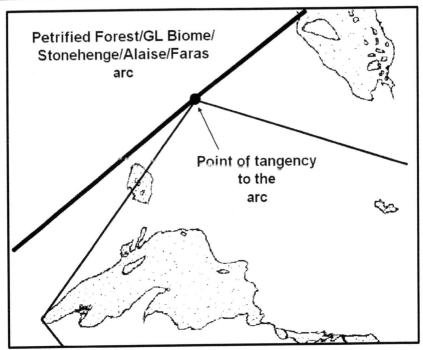

Petrified Forest/GL Biome/
Stonehenge/Alaise/Faras
arc

Point of tangency
to the
arc

POINT OF TANGENCY OF THE ALIGNMENT

In England, our path passes through the Perpetual Choirs Decagon. This set of alignments date from the Early Christian era, with Glastonbury cited as the original Christian site in England. However, the decagon also has roots at Stonehenge and other pre-Christian locations. This set of alignments includes monasteries and chapels, often built atop natural hills and mounds. As a decagon is evenly divisible by the number five, pentangles and pentagons similar to those of the Great Lakes can be inscribed into this system of alignments.

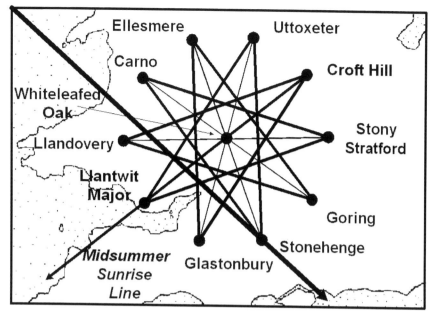

PATH THROUGH THE PERPETUAL CHOIRS DECAGON

In Southern England, we pass within one-tenth of a mile from the center of Stonehenge Circle.[95] One of the most easily recognized sites, in the world, Stonehenge is composed of earthworks that surround a circular setting of large standing stones. The site sits at the center of the densest complex of Neolithic and Bronze Age monuments in England, including several hundred burial mounds. Archaeologists believe that the iconic stone monument was erected in stages between 3000 and 2200 BCE. As with many of the sites that fall upon our alignments, Stonehenge has been recognized by the United Nations as a site of significance. UNESCO added Stonehenge and its surroundings to the list of World Heritage Sites in 1986. Note: As of 2008, Mike Parker Pearson, Professor of Archaeology at the University of Sheffield, England, had unearthed the foundations of more than 1,000 Neolithic houses in the vicinity of Stonehenge. His discoveries offer proof of the

---

[95] (51° 10' 44" N at 01° 49' 34" W)

existence of a thriving community at this location around 2500 BCE.

STONEHENGE—ACTUAL & IMAGINED RECONSTRUCTION

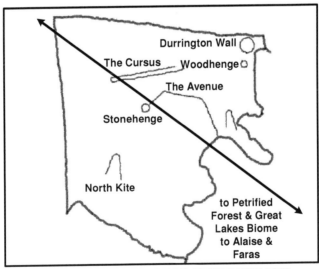

ALIGNMENT PASSING STONEHENGE

Continuing onward across the English Channel, we pass through France, traveling through the center of the Alaise Alignments within three miles of the village of Alaise. From this key point, we proceed through the base camps of the Matterhorn Mountain in Switzerland. The eastern face of the mountain is unusually curved and smooth. As the sun rises, the progressive golden glow on the face of the Matterhorn creates a bright natural landmark that can be observed from hundreds of miles away.

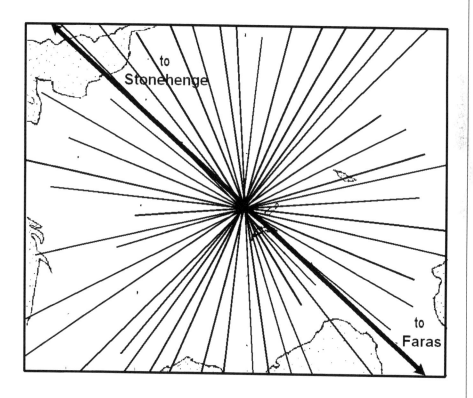

ALIGNMENT THROUGH ALAISE SYSTEM IN EUROPE

Passing the Matterhorn and progressing down through Italy, we cross the Mediterranean Sea. As we enter Egypt, we complete this leg of our journey at the site of Faras. Known in ancient times as Pachoras, Faras was a major city in Lower Nubia, which is now a part of modern Egypt.

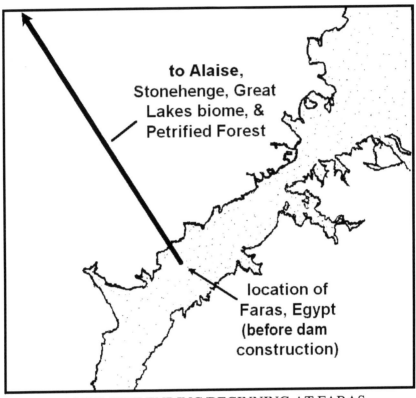

to Alaise, Stonehenge, Great Lakes biome, & Petrified Forest

location of Faras, Egypt (before dam construction)

ALIGNMENT ENDING/BEGINNING AT FARAS
ALONG THE NILE

Located slightly south of the great temple of Abu Simbel, Faras was a holy city of the ancient Egyptians that included the Ballana burial mounds. Though Abu Simbel was preserved by moving the entire structure to higher ground when the Aswan High Dam was constructed in the 1960s, the remains of Faras lie under the waters of the Nile.

CARVINGS AT ABU SIMBEL: RAMESSES II TEMPLE

The construction of the Abu Simbel temple complex, known originally as the "Temple of Ramesses, beloved by Amun," began in 1244 BCE and lasted for approximately twenty years. The complex received its new name from the legend that "Abu Simbel" was the name of a young local boy who had seen the monuments from time to time in the shifting sands and guided nineteenth-century explorers to the site of the buried temple. Eventually, the archeologists named the complex after him.

In 1959, international donations began to save the Nubian monuments. The rising waters of the Nile that resulted from the construction of the Aswan High Dam threatened these southernmost relics of an ancient human civilization.

Workers cut the entire temple site into large blocks. They then dismantled and reassembled it in a new location, sixty-five meters higher and 200 meters further back from the river. Many consider this feat as one of the greatest in the field of archaeological engineering. In addition, this effort even saved some structures that were under the waters of Lake Nasser.

Having completed this arc that aligns a number of significant world sites, let us return to the Great Lakes Biome for a wider view of everything that we have diagrammed. This view includes our new line that extends from the Petrified Forest in Arizona through the Great Lakes Biome, Stonehenge, and Alaise Alignments and terminates finally at Faras, Egypt.

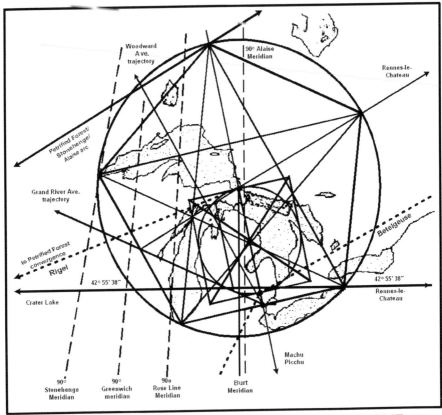

CURIOUS ALIGNMENTS OF THE GREAT LAKES BIOME

Chapter 20
CURIOSITY ONE

If we zoom out further, we can see the larger picture of these curious alignments. Let us draw a line from Mount Shasta down to the Nazca plateau in Peru. This line passes through the regions of Mexico and Central America that contain numerous Incan and Mayan cities, temples, and pyramids. When we arrive at the Nazca plateau, we find that one of the principal Nazcan lines points directly back to the peak of Mount Shasta in California, a mountain that a number of spiritual groups have considered as sacred throughout the ages.

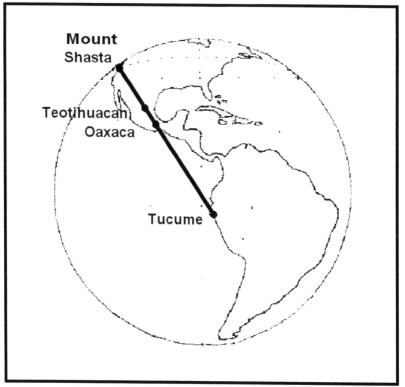

CORRIDOR OF PYRAMIDS

If we draw two lines from the peak of Mount Shasta, one to the Nazcan Lines and the other to Machu Picchu (each a length of about 4,900 miles), we will create a narrow corridor that contains four major pyramid groups: Caral, Tucume, Mitla/Oaxaca, and Teotihuacan. Over a length of 4,250 miles, the last three line up closely with one another and with Mount Shasta—curious, indeed.

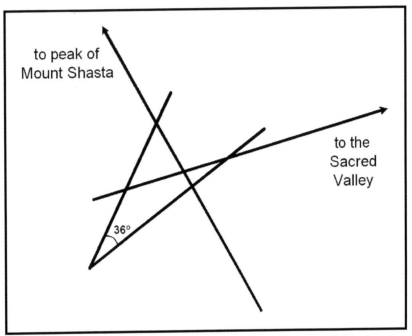

PRINCIPAL LINES AT NAZCA, PERU

Following another of the dominant Nazcan lines eastward takes us directly to the Sacred Valley of the Incas. Best known for its series of agricultural steps, this valley forms part of a larger pattern of Incan sites within the Machu Picchu "system."

STEPS OF THE SACRED VALLEY

The Machu Picchu System:

The Machu Picchu system of alignments includes twelve major sites, including Nazca:

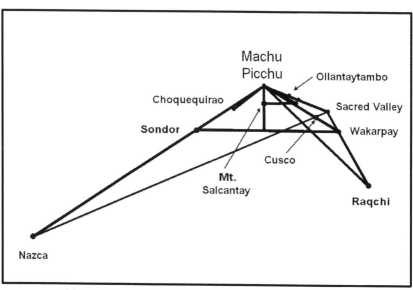

SYSTEM OF THE MACHU PICCHU ALIGNMENTS

Machu Picchu ("Old Peak") is an ancient holy site that the Incans eventually developed into a mountaintop royal retreat. Meghan A. Porter of the Minnesota State University E-Museum (mnsu.edu/emuseum, 2008) states that most likely Machu Picchu served as a religious retreat and royal estate. Comprising 200 buildings, the "modern" stone city was built between 1460 and 1470 CE by Incan ruler Pachacuti Inca Yupanqui. At an altitude of 8,000 feet, high above the cloud forest in the Urubamba River canyon, it probably did not serve any administrative, military, or commercial use. The architects of Machu Picchu used granite blocks, which they cut with bronze or stone tools, smoothed with sand, and fitted together without mortar. This represents a significant accomplishment, given that some blocks have as many as thirty corners. Similar to the Egyptian pyramids at Giza, the joints are so tight that even the thinnest of knife blades cannot be forced between the stones.

MACHU PICCHU IN 1911 CE

Choquequirao (Cradle of Gold) stands as a partly excavated ruined city. Referred to as the "sister" to Machu Picchu, this

148

Incan city bears a striking similarity to Machu Picchu in structure and architecture.

The ruins at Sondor Apurimac/Chanka remain a site of archeological investigation. Sondor ("Sitio Inca"--the Inca Place) served as a ceremonial center. According to studies, it has architectonical elements of monumental character. Five hundred steps up on the top of the central pyramid of the Muyu Muyu Ruins stands the sacred promontory of Sondor. Above the stairs and restored terraces, we find the Huaca, a sacred ritual site where human sacrifices presumably took place.

Salcantay Mountain rises as the highest peak of the Cordillera Vilcabamba, a segment of the Peruvian Andes chain. Located in the Cusco Region twelve miles due south of Machu Picchu, Salcantay is the thirty-eighth highest peak in the Andes and the twelfth highest one in Peru. However, as a high point in a range of deeply incised terrain, it appears as the second most prominent peak in the country.

The Ollantaytambo Ruins once served as the royal estate of Emperor Pachacuti, who conquered the region and built the town and ceremonial center. At the time of the Spanish Conquest, the estate served as a stronghold for Manco Inca Yupanqui, the leader of the Incan resistance.

OLLANTAYTAMBO

Atardecer en las Salineras de Maras is an ancient salt works that continues to serve the region in this capacity.

SALT WORKS

Moray is noted for a large complex of unusual Incan ruins. These include several enormous, terraced, circular depressions that the indigenous culture may have used to study the effects of climatic conditions on crops. The depth of the pits creates a temperature gradient of as much as 15° Centigrade between the top and the bottom. As with many other Incan sites, Moray possesses a highly sophisticated irrigation system for providing water to the plants.

MORAY "AMPHITHEATER"

Tambomachay/Cusco: Tambomachay ("resting place") is an Incan archaeological site on the hillside east of Cusco, Peru. It maintains an alternate local name of El Baño del Inca ("The Bath of the Inca"). The bath consists of a series of aqueducts, canals, and waterfalls running through the terraced rocks. Apart from serving as a spa resort for the Incan political elite, it may have served as a military outpost, guarding the approaches to Cusco.

TAMBOMACHAY

The original Incan city of Cusco, said to have been founded in the eleventh century CE, was sacked by the Spanish conquistador Pizarro in 1535. Remains of the Palace of the Incas, the Temple of the Sun, and the Temple of the Virgins of the Sun survive to this day. In many instances, the original Incan buildings only serve as the foundations for post-Incan structures.

CUSCO—TEMPLE OF THE SUN

The Sacred Valley perhaps is best known for Inca Písac, the Incan ruins which lie atop a hill at the entrance to the valley. Separated along the ridge into four groups, these ruins include Pisaqa, Intihuatana, Q'allaqasa, and Kinchiracay. The Temple of the Sun, a carved volcanic outcrop, forms the focal point of the valley. The angles of its base suggest that it served some astronomical function for the Incas.

Lining the hillside, the agricultural terraces constructed by the Inca are still used today. These terraces enable the population to produce more food than would be possible normally at a high altitude of 11,000 feet. Evidence in the form of military, religious, and agricultural structures suggests that the site served multiple purposes.

THE SACRED VALLEY OF THE INCAS

Pikillacta, so named as "City of Fleas" after the arrival of the Spanish and known today as Wakarpay, constitutes a large pre-Incan Huari archaeological site southeast of Cusco. Dating from 700 to 1000 CE, possibly was known earlier as Muyuna ("going around in circles"). The site remains one of the best maintained pre-Incan cities in Peru. Throughout the ruins, which feature empty streets, gigantic plazas, two-story palaces, and family housing, hundreds of lizards scuttle around.

Raqchi, an Incan archaeological site in the Cusco region, also is known as the Temple of Wiracocha. The remains of an enormous rectangular two-story roofed structure that measures 300 feet by eighty-four feet, the temple stands as the most prominent structure at the site. It consists of a central adobe wall with an andesitic base. A row of eleven columns flanks the remains on each side. The foundations of the walls and the columns exemplify classic, high-Incan stonework. Archeologists believe that the temple had the largest single roof in the Incan

Empire. The roof probably peaked at the central wall, stretched over the outer columns, and extended eighty-two feet beyond the walls on each side.

The Nazca Desert is a high, arid plateau that stretches thirty-seven miles on the Pampas de Jumana, Nazca is home to the mysterious and remarkable Nazca Lines. This plateau includes many geometric patterns as well as giant earth drawings of animals and other shapes believed to have been created by the Nazcan culture between 200 BCE and 600 CE. The site contains hundreds of individual figures that range in complexity from simple lines to stylized hummingbirds, spiders, monkeys, fish, sharks or orcas, llamas, and lizards. Scholars generally have ascribed religious significance to these figures. Other explanations offered include irrigation schemes, giant astronomical calendars, or landing strips for airships. One plausible explanation for the construction methods employed involves the use of simple surveying devices and other tools. A wooden stake that was found in the ground at the end of some lines serves to carbon-date the figures and supports this theory.

NAZCAN MONKEY

Lake Titicaca:

What we have referred to as the Machu Picchu system is a latter development within the region. It remains 300 miles northwest of a much older civilization centered at Lake Titicaca. This area contains Tiwanaku, a site recognized by Andean scholars as one of the most important precursors to the Incan civilization.

Also in Lake Titicaca we find Isla del Sol, an island that contains more than 180 ruins. Though most of the structures date to the era of the Inca, archeologists have discovered evidence that people lived on the island as early as the third millennium BCE. In the religion of the Incas, it was believed that the sun god was born on Isla del Sol, the Island of the Sun.

Chapter 21
CURIOSITY TWO

Extending lines from Machu Picchu to the intersections of the four European meridians at the 42° 55′ 38″N parallel produces some interesting results. From Machu Picchu, these lines connect with the Stonehenge, Greenwich, Paris (in the Rennes-le-Chateau geometry), and Alaise meridians. In itself, this observation has little meaning as we could connect these four meridians along that parallel to any given point in the world.

However, what raises a bit of intrigue in this exploration is the fact that these four lines pass through an area in the Atlantic Ocean that contains a large plateau and what appears to be a rectangular grid of trenches, roads, or some other unknown geometric "construction."[96] The plateau is known as the Great Meteor Tablemount (Seewart Seamounds). The grid rests on the floor of the Canary Basin and Madeira Plain. The rectangular grid of numerous parallel east-west and north-south lines forms an area of approximately eighty by 100 miles. This grid, which lies due south of the Azores, fits the longitude that David Wood asserts to be the location of Atlantis.

Furthermore, the line that extends from Machu Picchu through the center of this undersea grid proceeds directly to the junction of the Paris meridian at Rennes-le-Chateau parallel, a key point in the sacred geometric pattern of the Languedoc region of France. Similarly, extending a line westward from the tip of one of the north-south gridlines so that it parallels the lateral lines takes us directly to Teotihuacan, the Pyramid of the Sun. This pyramid is located 4,667 miles to the west by northwest from the undersea grid.

---

[96] at 31o 23′ 31″ N at 24o 19′ 20″ W

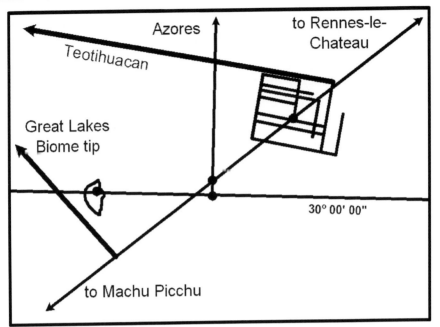

Azores

Teotihuacan

to Rennes-le-Chateau

Great Lakes Biome tip

30° 00' 00"

to Machu Picchu

MID-ATLANTIC PLAIN SOUTH OF THE AZORES

Chapter 22
CURIOSITY THREE

Numerous sacred sites appear along thirty degrees latitude north. These include the eastern corner of the configuration of Buddhist Sacred Mountains in China, sacred sites in Persia, and the Pyramids at Giza in Egypt.

Furthest to the east we find Mount Putuo, an island located to the southeast of Shanghai, China, that is named for a revered Bodhisattva. Chinese Buddhists consider Putuo to be motivated by compassion and to seek enlightenment, not only for him/herself but for everyone. Mount Putuo is one of the four sacred mountains in Chinese Buddhism, the others being Wutai, Jiuhua, and Emei.

Proceeding through the region of the sacred mountains and the Chinese mound pyramids (discussed in Chapter Twenty-Three), we continue westward through India, south of a number of sacred sites until we reach ancient Persia in Asia Minor.

In this region, we find the remains of the Sassanian, Parthian, and earlier Middle Eastern cultures. At Naqsh-e Rustam, an archaeological site just northwest of Persepolis, Iran,[97] we find a grotto that contains massive carved reliefs. In the most famous relief, Ardashir, the founder of the Sassanid Empire, is seen being handed the ring of kingship by Ahura Mazda, the Zoroastrian deity of light. In the inscription, which also bears the oldest attested use of the term "Iran," Ardashir admits to betraying his pledge to Artabanus V (the Persians having been a vassal state of the Arsacid Parthians). However, Ardashir legitimizes his action on the grounds that Ahura Mazda had willed it.

The statues were carved in the Sassanid art form. Though the figure on the left reflects a more modern depiction of a Sassanid

---

[97] (29° 59' 18" N at 52° 52' 21" E, .94 mi south of 30° 00' 00" N)

king, the figure on the far right contains features from the earlier culture of Persopolis. Note: the Persians have never had a visual depiction of Ahura Mazda.

INVESTITURE OF ARDASHIR I

Within the same neighborhood, we find the Ka'ba-i Zartosht ("Cube of Zoroaster"). This stone structure is a copy of a sister building at Pasargadae that was built between 521 and 338 BCE. Some archeologists believe that this copy was built as a safety box for the paraphernalia of the rulers in the vicinity of Persepolis. From a reference to fire altars in a Sassanid-era inscription on the building, it appears that the structure was once a fire altar or an eternal-flame memorial to the emperors whose tombs are located a few meters away. However, many deem this theory to be highly unlikely since the lack of cross-ventilation soon would have choked the flame.

Continuing further west, we pass through the heart of the ancient Nabataean Kingdom about twenty miles south of Petra, the city carved out of the cliff walls in Jordan. The city of Petra is an archaeological site lying on the slope of Mount Hor in a basin among the mountains that form the eastern flank of Arabah, the large valley running from the Dead Sea to the Gulf of Aqaba. The city is renowned for its rock-cut architecture. Petra was constructed by the Nabateans, an Aramaic-speaking Semite people, in approximately 100 BCE. The Nabateans built it as the capital city at the center of their caravan trade route. Designated as a World Heritage Site in 1985, Petra was described by UNESCO as "one of the most precious cultural properties of man's cultural heritage."

PETRA TREASURY

The Great Pyramid of Giza, also called Khufu's Pyramid and the Pyramid of Cheops, is the oldest and largest of the three pyramids in the Giza Necropolis. It borders what is now Cairo, Egypt.[98] The Great Pyramid remains the only surviving site of the Seven Wonders of the Ancient World. Believed to have been built as a tomb for Khufu (Cheops in Greek), an Egyptian king who lived in the fourth dynasty, it was constructed over a twenty-year period that concluded around 2560 BCE. The Great Pyramid was the tallest man-made structure in the world for over 3,800 years.

PYRAMIDS AT GIZA, EGYPT

Originally, the builders covered the Great Pyramid with casing stones that formed a smooth outer surface. Today, we see only the underlying core structure. Some of the casing stones that once covered the structure still remain around the base. Various scientific and alternative theories have prevailed, regarding the construction techniques used to build the Great Pyramid. Most of the accepted theories revolve around the idea that it was built by moving huge stones from a quarry and dragging and lifting them into place.

---

[98] (29° 58′ 45″ N, 31° 08′ 04″ E, 1.5 mi S of 30° 00′ 00″ N)

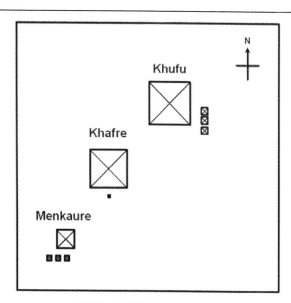

PYRAMIDS AT GIZA

Chapter 23
CURIOSITY FOUR

The alignment that begins and ends at Machu Picchu, Peru, and passes through the Great Lakes Biome continues over the top of the world. Traveling this path downward into China takes us into the midst of the five Taost Sacred Mountains, the Four Buddhist Sacred Mountains, and the Chinese Pyramids near the city of Xi'an.

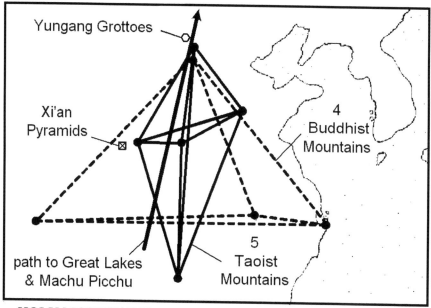

HOLY MOUNTAINS, GROTTOES & PYRAMIDS OF CHINA

According to Chinese Taoist mythology, the Five Great Mountains originated from the limbs and head of Pangu, the first being and creator of the world. The Five Great Mountains are arranged according to the five cardinal directions of Chinese geomancy. By orientation, these include: East—Tai Shan, "Leading Peaceful Mountain," West—Hua Shan, "Splendid Mountain," South—Nan Heng Shan, "Balancing Mountain,"

165

North—Bei Heng Shan, "Permanent Mountain," and Center—Song Shan, "Lofty Mountain."

SHAOLIN MONASTERY AT SONG SHAN

Because of its eastern location, Taoists associate Mount Tài with the rising sun, the symbol of birth and renewal. As a result, they often regard it as the most sacred of the Five Great Mountains, believing it to have been formed out of Pangu's head.

To Buddhists, mountains are where Heaven and Earth touch. They believe that Bodhisatvas--Buddhist disciples who have reached nirvana but have come back to Earth to help mortals on their own paths to enlightenment--dwell in four sacred mountains. Over the centuries, Buddhist monasteries have built large complexes at these sacred peaks.

For Buddhists, the Four Sacred Mountains in China include: Wutai Shan—"Five-Terrace Mountain," Emei Shan—"Delicate-Eyebrow Mountain," Jiuhua Shan—"Nine-Glories Mountain," and Putuo Shan—"Potalaka Mountain."

SHRINE ATOP A HOLY MOUNTAIN

Along the alignment of Machu Picchu and the Soo, we find the Yungang Grottoes, the ancient Buddhist temple grottoes in the Chinese province of Shanxi. Collectively, these rock-cut architecture grottoes are one of the three most famous ancient sculptural sites of China, the others being Longmen and Mogao.

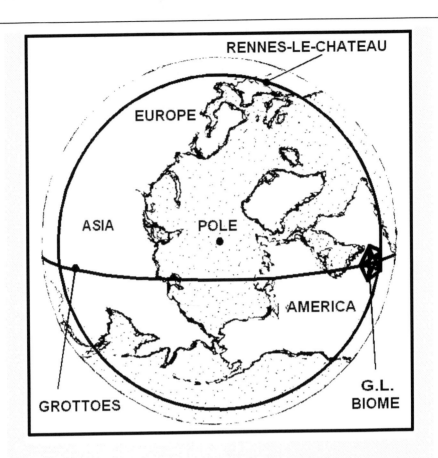

MACHU PICCHU—SOO—YUNGANG GROTTOES ALIGNMENT

The Yungang site is located in the valley of the Shi Li River at the base of the Wutai Shan Mountains. Mainly, the 252 grottoes, with their more than 51,000 Buddha statues and statuettes, were constructed between 460 and 525 CE during the Northern Wei dynasty.

YUNGANG GROTTOES ALONG
THE SOO-MACHU PICCHU ALIGNMENT

The Longmen Grottoes (aka Dragon's Gate Grottoes) stand in the Henan province of China. Carved between 316 and 907 CE, the grottoes, which overwhelmingly depict Buddhist subjects, dot the faces of the Xiangshan and Longmenshan (mountains), with the Yi River flowing between them. Over 2,100 niches, more than 100,000 statues, forty pagodas, and 3,600 tablets and steles are in the caves. Located near the Shaolin monastery and the Song Mountain, these grottoes represent the most impressive collection of Chinese art from this period.

LONGMEN GROTTO NEAR SONG MOUNTAIN

Near the western end of the sacred mountain region of China, about 100 miles from the Machu Picchu-Soo alignment extending into China, we find a large complex of pyramids. These so-called pyramids of China are actually ancient mausoleums and burial mounds. Approximately thirty eight of them are located northwest of Xi'an on the Qin Chuan Plains. The most famous is the Mausoleum of the First Qin Emperor, located northeast of Xi'an near the location of the Army of Terracotta Warriors. Interestingly, many of these mounds have flat tops. More than resembling the pyramids in Giza, they embody the shape of the Teotihuacan Pyramid of the Sun, northeast of Mexico City along the Nazca-Mount Shasta alignment.

The 2,000 year old Maoling Mausoleum is composed of densely packed earth. It stands as the largest and most impressive of eleven Western-Han imperial mausoleums and serves as the final resting place of Emperor Liu Che, who reigned from 157 to 87 BCE. Chinese history tells us that the tomb took fifty-three years to complete and was filled with precious burial objects, some of which have avoided plundering and are on display at a nearby museum. In addition, we find the burial mound of Emperor Qin Shi Huang, who unified the country in 221 BCE. In *Records of the Grand Historian: Biography of Qin Shi Huang* (109-91 BCE), historian Sima Qian describes a burial chamber that contains miniature palaces and pavilions with flowing rivers and surging oceans of mercury lying beneath a ceiling decorated in jewels depicting the sun, moon and stars.

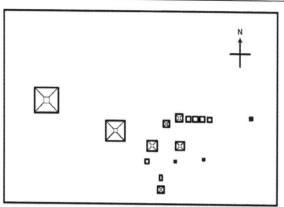

PYRAMIDS OF YA SEN PARK NEAR XI'AN

Chapter 24
WRAPPING IT UP
(LIKE A BALL OF TWINE)

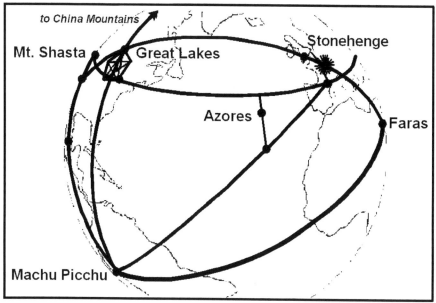

MAJOR ALIGNMENTS DISCOVERED TO DATE

In terms of curious alignments and sacred places, what we have discovered may be only a small piece of the whole picture. The entire system of sites and alignments may be much more complex. Then again, perhaps what we have just seen is nothing more than a collection of "Curious Alignments." If not, then we must answer a number of questions. These include, but are not limited to,

- What is the significance of these discoveries?
- Were all the ancient civilizations interconnected here on earth and elsewhere?
- Can we use these sites again and for what?
- Does the interconnectivity of sites suggest that all the religions were set up from a common advanced intelligence?

In the fall of 2009, my Urban Economics students viewed and listened to a three-hour PowerPoint presentation of *Curious Alignments*. In addition, they read the working draft of this book. As part of a class assignment, I asked them to write out questions and comments in response to what they viewed, heard, and read.

The following pages contain some of their responses. Their thoughts will certainly influence my further research.

Questions and Comments from
Economics and Urban Studies Students

1. Do you believe that it would have been more beneficial for the builders and city planners to concentrate more on other factors such as geology, topography, and population sustainability instead of trying to align their creations with the great civilization centers of the time?

2. Do you think that it is more likely that ancient cities were trading with each other and building their cities with these alignments in mind, or did the cities end up being built this way due to every ancient civilization studying the stars and using their paths and blueprints?

3. I went to Athens, Greece, this past summer. I was wondering if ever during your work you found anything significant regarding the Acropolis. Maybe the various historical landmarks throughout Athens make their own curious alignments.

4. My question about the curious alignments is whether or not the landmark locations of the various people of the Earth are powered by a cosmic force that mankind has yet to understand? Could it be possible that the movements of the planets and stars affect the decisions of mankind in a way that modern society has yet to understand or, in some ways, lost touch with?

5. How would the extraction and transport of these [copper] deposits have been possible at that time? It seems that the

travel time and the weight would have been a significant deterrent. Do the alignments suggest some kind of travel route?

6. While much evidence exists that copper was being mined in the Lake Superior region thousands of years ago and that copper was being traded among the indigenous peoples in the American northeast, only the controversial Peterborough petroglyphs seem to indicate any European contact before Norsemen explored Newfoundland around 1000 CE. Given that the discovery of the largest deposit of native copper in the world would have been of vast importance to Bronze Age Europeans, what explanations have you unearthed for the archaeological gap between the possible initial contact circa 1500 BCE and what we know about the later Norse exploration?

7. Is it possible that our Creator wanted his people to develop their minds and obtain knowledge strategically and put these alignments into place? Also, is it possible that at every point that the pentagon touches, something, that our minds can't even foresee, will happen at these points? Pentagons are known for protection of some sort. Could this pentagon shape be purposely constructed throughout the Earth for protection of the people?

8. Design of the recent past seems to be based on location to resources, economic gain, and cheap land rather than meaningful patterns that would further the sacred and divine. We get our answers from books and scientists. Do you think that we have moved away from ancient thoughts with new technology, new ideas, and individual gain over community gain, etc.? If not, then why?

9. With our current technology, we can easily see two locations using an overview map from Google Earth. So, we can easily connect two locations with a straight line. How did the pre-historic people connect two locations that were far distant from each other if they did not have an overview map of the Earth?

10. My knowledge of astronomy is not very extensive. However, would it be possible to try to take the alignments you've

shown on the maps and somehow relate them to the sky, like you did with Orion? In addition to the details of Scared Geometry and astronomical occurrence that connect these lines, drawing conclusions with what is outside of this planet could be an important contribution to your book. Now all you need is Google Universe.

11. Couldn't this be why all of these different cultures have important monuments built along certain latitudes and longitudes? If this is the case, is the thought behind going in depth with the charts and graphs just to demonstrate which structures were built where? Or, are we still trying to get a grasp of a "bigger picture?"

12. Could the Michigan Mounds, and the way upon which people worshipped, have contributed to the downturn of Detroit? The Great Mound of the Rouge was used for burial practices. It was 400 feet long, 200 feet wide, and forty feet high. It was packed with bones that were easily exposed by wandering cattle. Why weren't these ancient people given a decent burial instead of a mass grave? Could this be a place of unrest where evil lurks? It is no secret that Detroit has had its ups and downs--or maybe there is a secret? Why haven't these mounds been preserved, exhibited and toured like other civilizations so that we may learn more about our ancestors?

13. Our common thought on ancient civilizations, as taught in most schools, was that they were generally geocentric and focused on survival and proliferation of their own communities. Your findings suggest quite the opposite, that these populations around the world had some kind of knowledge or awareness of each other. Given the lack of technology of the era, does this suggest that a "higher power" influenced the placements of mounds and monuments?

14. Some points are natural formations, others are religious places, and a few others are cities. Most originated at different periods of time, even in the same alignment. Do you believe that the inconsistent form of the points reduces the significance of your findings? Is it possible that if an alignment was found that was of a uniform composition that it would have superior importance?

15. From the presentation of *Curious Alignments,* I have gathered that the Earth's surface has specific points of high energy, as illustrated by the Sedona Vortices. These points were often co-opted by the religious hierarchy, of the time period, that thus erected numerous holy sites, temples, churches, and other culturally significant developments atop these specific points. As the natural oscillations of the Earth slowly shifted, these points of high energy also moved in conjunction with Earth's own magnetic field. Could these points of high energy be affected not only by the Earth's magnetic field, but also the energy field of the sun? Could these forces be shown to affect the behavior of people?

16. Did the Mayans, for example, build the pyramids at Comalcalco, which are made of clay mixed with sand and dried oyster shells, out of their own free will for the sake of worship and gratitude to their gods, or were they enslaved and forced to do so? Could it be possible that the Pyramid of the Sun at Teotihuacan, Mexico, and that of the Cheops Pyramid at Giza are identical because the people of those ancient times were nomadic and therefore traveled for exploratory purposes?

17. What is the importance of delegating sacred geometry? Was it an attempt to unite civilizations of the world through a constant representation of the divine? Or could it be a natural tool, such as a map, that allowed people to trustfully navigate thousands of miles of land or sea?

18. The alignment of structures with the Orion Constellation appears several places throughout the world at different times, in different cultures, and in different parts of the world. Is there deeper significance to the stars that make up Orion's Belt that make them more often repeated than those of the rest of the constellation?

19. The major avenues of Detroit, such as Woodward and Grand River Avenues pass across the midpoints of the sides of the inscribed pentagons of the Great Lakes circle. Did the urban street development of Detroit invisibly follow the principle of compatibility with the Great Lakes areas so that it became a regional city?

20. Do you believe that some ancient structures could have been built in certain alignments to mask or unmask secrets of an ancient civilization? Do you think that maybe some of these structures and their alignments, in accordance possibly with the sun, stars, other planets, and the moon, could be used to lead to a secret area or city to where a civilization would flee in times of distress and survive—a place so well hidden that we have yet to discover it?

21. You admit that the Michigan-Ohio region is littered with burial mounds, which makes it easy to believe that many of these mounds line up in geometric shapes. What percentage of the mounds in the region line up in a significant way? If a majority of them do, then it would seem to be more than just coincidence.

22. If you are arguing that the placement of the Pyramids of Giza, Machu Picchu, and the burial mounds of Ohio and Michigan are all interrelated, does that mean that all civilizations believed in a common religion? Or, could it be that these people were engaging in communication, and if so how? Also, if you are trying to get us to think about economics and transaction through knowledge spillovers or exchange, how did these ancient civilizations conduct or interact, based on the latitudinal or longitudinal alignments, and what role did they play in fostering these unusual alignments? Do you believe that there is a contextual link to the ancient alignments and modern urban economics? If so, what is the link?

23. Besides alignments, are there recurring themes with the mounds that link them together? Can you explain how you think that the mounds in Ohio may relate to the lost Incan city? Additionally, what does the line between these two points relate/correspond to, or point to, if anything?

24. In the book, you focus on how the copper mines line up. Do any other major natural resources such as gold, silver, or even oil have curious alignments? In so, which ones? Also, if none of these other natural resources have these curious alignments, why is copper the only one with a curious alignment? Is there something about copper that makes it different from other natural resources?

25. The research brings a holistic understanding of the geography of the world and shows the global awareness that was once lost, only to be "rediscovered" by Western Civilization in the past 500 years. In understanding the deeper implications and movements of societies of the past, what can we do to reconnect to these common roots? Once we understand the connectedness of cultures, people, and common history that we share as a human race, what can we do today to reconnect?

26. While I was wondering what these alignments could be caused by, if not direct contact between distant cultures, I was reminded of another of your presentations--the video on ferrofluids. I thought of it not only because of the patterns that the fluids create are often similar to the alignments, but also because it reminded me of the "energy vortex" mentioned in the text and a possible connection to the Earth's magnetic fields. Could these fields have had some subconscious effects on human behavior that resulted in some of the alignments? Many birds are able to perceive the Earth's magnetic fields and use this ability for migration. Some studies have shown also that humans have some degree of what is called "magnetoreception," though they typically aren't conscious of it. Could these things be related to the alignments? What implications might this have?

27. There are questions about what these findings mean. One who is unfamiliar with this subject might ask roughly, what portion of the total holy/sacred sites, ancient wonders, and burial mounds are found along these lines? Likely, there are important sites to be found outside of these alignments. Does this detract from the meaningfulness of these observations?

28. If different civilizations built structures and cities with intended alignments for similar religious or spiritual purposes, what accounts for the variation among the different religious interpretations and beliefs that the cultures eventually developed?

29. Is it possible that some of these alignments may have been created as trails or paths between civilizations that could be followed in the same way that they were built, through the sun and stars? This information might not have been passed

down to everyone due to the fact that if enemy civilizations were to obtain it, it might make it easier for them to attack if they had a path that they could follow at night. If this were true, do you think that this could be a reason as to why these paths were never documented and may have only been passed along by word of mouth?

30. After reading the text and watching the slide show, one thought that comes to my mind is a spiritual meaning to all of these alignments and how they connect. Our early ancestors were able to compute this Sacred Geometry and, as we know, many believed in a higher being. Is it possible that the pentagon, also being the shape that sound travels through a room, is the way communication will take place when the world is ending and Jesus comes back?

31. I would like to find out if any of the early civilizations have connections with the Greeks. They are known in history as great architects and developers of early forms of geometry. I have noticed in *Curious Alignments* that there isn't any mention of any Greek architecture. I haven't been able to use Google Earth to connect the dots. So, I was wondering if there is some way that there could be a connection with other early civilizations.

32. When mankind was able to closely guess the size of the Earth, could it have been possible that there was cooperation between different states at the time in order to help to get a valid estimate? Could it have been possible that the Norsemen, who came into the Lake Superior area to take copper long ago might have traded or dealt with the Egyptians who needed the copper to build their historical monuments? Is it possible that the Egyptians might have shared some of their techniques with the Peruvians, or vice versa, through Norseman mediation since the former had a huge copper resource and the latter was in need of it?

33. The alignments do not surprise me. I approach life with a biblical perspective and evidence of city building civilization is presented in the biblical account of the Tower of Babel. The book of Genesis states that all men descended from Noah's line as his line is all that survived the flood which occurs in

Genesis. Through the generations, his descendents increase in number and, by Genesis: 11, his descendents planned to build a city of brick instead of stone, using tar for mortar, as well as a city with a tower that reached to the heavens. In all likelihood, this tower was what we have come to call a ziggurat. They would have been successful. However, God confused the language of man which caused them to separate, most likely along kin lines. If this is taken as literal history, then it would explain why we see these same patterns and alignments throughout the world. It seems like common sense that if two groups navigate by the stars an also build cities according to astronomical alignments, that they would align and use many of the same patterns. I do not believe that each civilization that resulted from the events at the Tower of Babel retained all of the skills of the original civilization. A loss in skill and information is not unheard of, as the Dark Ages occurred after the collapse of the Roman Empire. I believe that a grandfather civilization is the cause of these patterns.

PHOTO AND ILLUSTRATION CREDITS

1. THE ROSELINE AT SAINT SULPICE/stockxpert.com/Albo
2. REMAINS OF THE TEMPLE OF THE SUN AT CUZCO/public domain
3. STANDING STONES OF STENNESS/istockphoto.com/Henry Chaplin
4. MISSISSIPPI MOUNDS/author's rendering
5. AVEBURY HENGE/istockphoto.com/Jason Mooy
6. STONEHENGE/istockphoto.com/Roberto Gennaro
7. RAISING LINTELS AT STONEHENGE/author's rendering
8. PYRAMID BUILDING/author's rendering
9. SETTING STONES ON THE PYRAMIDS/author's rendering
10. MAP OF HOCHELAGA/public domain
11. HOPEWELL MOUND CITY/public domain/author's rendering
12. MOUND CITY AND THE GREAT MOUND OF THE ROUGE/author's rendering
13. EASTERN MICHIGAN MOUND GROUPS/author's rendering
14. MICHIGAN AND OHIO OVERVIEW/author's rendering
15. CONNECTIONS TO ATLANTA AND MACHU PICCHU/author's rendering
16. THE CONSTELLATION ORION/author's rendering
17. BOYNTON CANYON/istockphoto.com/Nathan Chor
18. SEDONA VORTICE ALIGNMENTS/author's rendering
19. THE ALAISE ALIGNMENTS OF XAVIER GUICHARD/public domain
20. FRANKISH EMPIRE WITH SUPERIMPOSED MERIDIANS/author's rendering
21. THE GREAT LAKES BIOME—PETER CHAMPOUX 2002/author's rendering
22. CENTER POINT AT THE SOO/author's rendering
23. THE SOO LOCKS—ORIGINAL/public domain
24. SOO LOCKS TODAY/istockphoto.com/Michael Westhoff
25. GEOMETRIC PLAN OF CENTRAL DETROIT 1805/public domain/author's rendering
26. THE LOST INCAN CITY OF MACHU PICCHU/istockphoto.com/Amy Harris
27. ALIGNMENT TO THE LARGE OUT-CROPPING/author's rendering
28. APPROXIMATE FORMER LOCATION OF THE MANITOU TOTEM/istockphoto.com/Gary Marx II
29. SOO – MACHU PICCHU LINE THROUGH DETROIT/author's rendering
30. THE THREE CIRCLE CENTERS AND DETROIT BASE POINT/author's rendering
31. MICHIGAN-OHIO MERIDIAN & RENNES-LE-CHATEAU ALIGNMENT/author's rendering
32. SOO-MACHU PICCHU ALIGNMENT/author's rendering
33. MAJOR DEPOSITS OF COPPER, GOLD & SILVER/author's rendering
34. THE FIRST CIRCLE/author's rendering
35. THE SECOND CIRCLE/author's rendering
36. THE THIRD CIRCLE/author's rendering
37. THE FOURTH AND FIFTH CIRCLES/author's rendering
38. VESICA PISCIS AS BALANCING CONSCIOUSNESS/author's rendering
39. THE FIRST EQUILATERAL TRIANGLE/author's rendering
40. THE SECOND TRIANGLE/author's rendering
41. THE EMERGENCE OF SOLOMON'S KEY/author's rendering
42. SOLOMON'S KEY/author's rendering
43. COMPLETING SOLOMON'S KEY/author's rendering
44. PHI/author's rendering

91. SALT WORKS/istockphoto.com/Antonio Salado Cano
92. MORAY "AMPHITHEATER"/istockphoto.com/Jarno Gonzalez Zarraona
93. TAMBOMACHAY/istockphoto.com/Jarno Gonzalez Zarraona
94. CUSCO—TEMPLE OF THE SUN/istockphoto.com/Yin Yang
95. THE SACRED VALLEY OF THE INCAS/ istockphoto.com/Jarno Gonzalez Zarraona
96. NAZCAN MONKEY/public domain
97. MID-ATLANTIC PLAIN SOUTH OF THE AZORES/author's rendering
98. INVESTITURE OF ARDASHIR I/wikimedia commons
99. PETRA TREASURY/istockphoto.com/Simon Podgorsek
100. PYRAMIDS AT GIZA, EGYPT/istockphoto.com/Volker Kreinacke
101. PYRAMIDS AT GIZA/author's rendering
102. HOLY MOUNTAINS, GROTTOES, & PYRAMIDS OF CHINA/author's rendering
103. SHAOLIN MONASTERY AT SONG SHAN/ istockphoto.com/KingWu
104. SHRINE ATOP A HOLY MOUNTAIN/istockphoto.com/George Clerk
105. MACHU PICCHU—SOO—YUNGANG GROTTOES ALIGNMENT/author's rendering
106. YUNGANG GROTTOES ALONG THE SOO-MACHU PICCHU ALIGNMENT/istockphoto.com/Cui Zhang
107. LONGMEN GROTTO NEAR SONG MOUNTAIN/istockphoto.com/David Kerkhoff
108. PYRAMIDS OF YA SEN PARK NEAR XI'AN/author's rendering
109. MAJOR ALIGNMENTS DISCOVERED TO DATE/author's rendering

SELECTED BIBLIOGRAPHY

Bairoch, Paul. *Cities and Economic Development: From the Dawn of History to the Present,* University of Chicago Press, 1991.

Champoux, Peter., and William Stuart Buehler. *Gaia Matrix: Arkhom & the Geometries of Destiny in the North American Landscape.* Franklin Media, 1999.

Drier, Roy W. "Archeology and Some Metallurgical Investigative Techniques." In *Lake Superior Copper and the Indians: Miscellaneous Studies of Great Lakes Prehistory,* ed. James B. Griffin. Anthropological Papers 17. Ann Arbor: Museum of Anthropology, University of Michigan, 1961.

Drier, Roy W., and Octave J. Du Temple, eds. *Prehistoric Copper Mining in the Lake Superior Region.* Calumet, MI and Hinsdale, IL, 1961.

Dunbar, Willis F., and George S. May. *Michigan: A History of the Wolverine State,* Wm. B. Eerdmans Publishing Company; Revised edition, 1980.

Farmer, Silas. *A History of Detroit and Michigan,* Farmer, 1884.

Fell, Barry. *America B.C.: Ancient Settlers in the NewWorld,* Pocket, 1979.

Fell, Barry. *Bronze Age America,* Little Brown & Co., 1982.

Haagensen, Erling, and Henry Lincoln. *The Templars' Secret Island: The Knights, the Priest, and the Treasure,* Barnes & Noble Books, 2004.

Hamlin, Marie Caroline Watson. *Legends of Le Detroit,* unknown, 1884. Reprinted by Cornell University Library, 2009.

Hawkins, Gerald S. *Stonehenge Decoded: An Astronomer Examines One of the Great Puzzles of the Ancient World,* Souvenir, 1966.

Heath, Robin and John Michell. *The Lost Science of Measuring the Earth: Discovering the Sacred Geometry of the Ancients,* Adventures Unlimited Press, 2006.

Hinsdale, W.B. *Archaeological Atlas of Michigan,* University of Michigan Press, 1931.

Hinsdale, W.B. *Primitive Man in Michigan,* unknown, 1925. Reprinted by Avery Color Studios, 1979.

Houghton, John Jacob. *The Ancient Copper Mines of Lake Superior,* included in the Collections of the State Historical Society of Wisconsin, Volume 8, 1879.

Hubbard, Bela. *Memorials of a Half Century,* 1887. Reprinted by the Gale Group, 1978.

Keating, William H. *Narrative of an Expedition to the Source of St. Peter's River, Lake Winnepeek, Lake of the Woods and c., Performed in the Year 1823.* Ross & Haines, 1959.

Lawlor, Robert. *Sacred Geometry: Philosophy and Practice,* Thames & Hudson, 1989.

Lincoln, Henry. *The Holy Place: Saunière and the Decoding of the Mystery of Rennes-le-Château,* Arcade, 2004.

Martin, Susan R. *Wonderful power: the story of ancient copper working in the Lake Superior Basin,* Wayne State University Press, 1999.

Michell, John. *Ancient Metrology: The Dimensions of Stonehenge and of the Whole World as Therein Symbolized,* Pentacle Books, 1981.

Modelski, George, *World Cities: 3000 to 2000,* FAROS2000, 2003.

Pawlicki, T. B. "Megalithic Engineering: How to Build Stonehenge and the Pyramids with Bronze Age Technology," in *How to Build a Flying Saucer and Other Proposals in Speculative Engineering,* Prentice Hall, 1981.

Qian, Sima and trans. Watson, Burton (1993), *Records of the Grand Historian: Han Dynasty.* Research Center for Translation, The Chinese University of Hong Kong and Columbia University Press.

Sase, John. *The Development Business Subcenters in Radial Monocentric Cities.* Doctoral dissertatation, Wayne State University, 1992.

Solis, Ruth Shady. *Caral: The City of the Sacred Fire.* Currently unavailable.

Wood, David. *Genisis: the First Book of Revelations,* Baton Press, 1986.

THE MYSTERY CONTINUES TO UNFOLD

Made in the USA
Lexington, KY
25 August 2010